PRAY
AS THEY PRAYED

A Guide to the Bible's Greatest Prayers

JEFF WELLS

LUCIDBOOKS

Pray as They Prayed
A Guide to the Bible's Greatest Prayers

Copyright © 2025 by Jeff Wells
Published by Lucid Books in Houston, TX
www.LucidBooks.com

All rights reserved. No part of this publication may be reproduced, stored in a retrieval system, or transmitted in any form by any means, electronic, mechanical, photocopy, recording, or otherwise, without the prior permission of the publisher, except as provided for by USA copyright law.

Unless otherwise indicated, scripture quotations are taken from the ESV® Bible (The Holy Bible, English Standard Version®), copyright © 2001 by Crossway, a publishing ministry of Good News Publishers. Used by permission. All rights reserved.

Scripture quotations marked (NIV) are taken from the Holy Bible, New International Version®, NIV®. Copyright ©1973, 1978, 1984, 2011 by Biblica, Inc.™ Used by permission of Zondervan. All rights reserved worldwide. www.zondervan.com The "NIV" and "New International Version" are trademarks registered in the United States Patent and Trademark Office by Biblica, Inc.™

ISBN: 978-1-63296-771-8
e:ISBN: 978-1-63296-772-5

Special Sales: Most Lucid Books titles are available in special quantity discounts. Custom imprinting or excerpting can also be done to fit special needs. Contact Lucid Books at Info@LucidBooks.com

I dedicate this book to the wonderful congregation of WoodsEdge Community Church. It has been my privilege to serve these dear people as pastor since 1993. I am especially grateful for their prayers for Gayle and me. WoodsEdge, we love you so much!

TABLE OF CONTENTS

Chapter 1: Nothing Is Too Hard — 1

Chapter 2: As Close As We Get — 7

Chapter 3: Not Desperate Enough — 15

Chapter 4: Show Me Your Glory — 19

Chapter 5: Listening Prayer — 25

Chapter 6: Learning to Hear God Better — 31

Chapter 7: Heart on Fire — 39

Chapter 8: A Plea for Prayer — 43

Chapter 9: Our Eyes Are On You — 51

Chapter 10: Passionate Love — 59

Chapter 11: The Language of Love — 63

Chapter 12: O Begin! — 69

Chapter 13: Daniel's Classic Prayer — 75

Chapter 14: Never Forget — 81

Chapter 15: God-Centered Prayer — 85

Chapter 16: The Heart of a Father — 89

Chapter 17: Ask! — 93

Chapter 18: The Secret Place	99
Chapter 19: Never Give Up!	105
Chapter 20: House of Prayer	109
Chapter 21: The Greater Work	115
Chapter 22: God Is Present	119
Chapter 23: Prayer and the Word	125
Chapter 24: Bold Prayer	131
Chapter 25: The 6:4 Calling	137
Chapter 26: Fervent United Prayer	141
Chapter 27: This Is How We Fight Our Battles	147
Chapter 28: Lifeblood	151
Chapter 29: The Prayer of Epaphras	155
Chapter 30: A Way of Life	159
Chapter 31: Thanksgiving	165
Chapter 32: Great Power	171
Appendix A: Classic Prayers	175
Appendix B: Praise Passages	183
Endnotes	185

Chapter 1

NOTHING IS TOO HARD

Is anything too hard for the Lord?
—Genesis 18:14

So many of our prayer requests seem impossible. We think to ourselves, "This will take a miracle."

A loved one has terminal cancer, and we are asking God for miraculous healing. Our spouse has struggled for years with debilitating depression, and we are praying for a breakthrough. We have a teenage son who has battled drug and alcohol addiction for several years, and we are desperate. Our eighty-three-year-old father has been hardened against the gospel, and we are crying out for salvation before he dies. Our closest friends have struggled with infertility for nine years, and we are begging God to give them children. For over thirty years we have been praying for genuine revival in our city and in our country.

For all these situations and more, God has stamped these words on my heart: *"Is anything too hard for the LORD?"* These words give us perspective on prayer. They come from Genesis 18:14 when God says to Sarah: *"Is anything too hard for the LORD?"* This is a question that I regularly revisit and repeat to myself.

Here's the background in Genesis 18. Abraham sits in the shade of his tent in the stifling desert heat. That's when he notices them: three men, just standing there. Compelled by Middle Eastern hospitality, Abraham scurries to serve his guests.

At some point, it becomes clear to Abraham that one of these men is none other than God himself—God in human form—and the other two are angels. God tells Abraham that his wife Sarah will give birth to a son *"about this time next year."* What makes this statement so stunning is that Abraham is ninety-nine years old, and Sarah is eighty-nine years old.

God had promised them, twenty-four years earlier, that they would have a child, but he never told them *when* that child would come. They had waited and waited . . . month after month, year after year. It would be understandable if Abraham and Sarah had given up on ever having their own child. But now, for the first time, God tells them *when* they will have a child—at this time next year.

Behind the tent curtains, Sarah is eavesdropping on the conversation. When she hears the statement about having a baby, she laughs to herself. She laughs to herself in unbelief. She is thinking: "I am eighty-nine years old, and there is no way that I am going to get pregnant and deliver a baby at ninety years of age. You have got to be kidding me!"

God, knowing all things, knows that Sarah laughed, and he knows *why* she laughed. He immediately responds, addressing Abraham:

> *Why did Sarah laugh and say, "Shall I indeed bear a child now that I am old." Is anything too hard for the Lord? At the appointed time I will return to you, about this time next year, and Sarah shall have a son.*
> —Genesis 18:13–14

God's question to Abraham *"Is anything too hard for the* Lord*?"* is emblazoned on my soul. It echoes in my heart. I cannot get away from it. This question regularly comes to my mind: *"Is anything too hard for the* Lord*?"*

The question answers itself immediately. And emphatically. How could anything be too hard for the sovereign, infinite, all-powerful God? If there was something too hard for God, something bigger than God could handle, then God would not be God. The God who created hundreds of billions of galaxies, with his mere breath, has all power and authority in the universe. He can do anything he wants to do. The God who raises the dead to life can take care of my biggest problem.

God is saying to Abraham and Sarah: "Yes, you, Sarah, are barren, and you are way past bearing a child. But I am the Lord God Almighty, Creator of the universe, and I can do this, no problem. And I will do this. And all the world down through history will know that this baby boy, Isaac, is a miracle baby. All the world will know that I am a miracle-working God and that nothing is too hard for the Lord!"

When it comes to prayer, we must put these words of God in the front of our brains and deep in our heart: "Nothing is too hard for the Lord!"

When I was four years old, I developed a health problem that was both serious and mysterious. I was taken to the massive New Orleans Baptist Hospital where doctors conducted tests in an attempt to diagnose the disease. They were speculating that it might be leukemia or Bright's Disease among other dark maladies. But they could not diagnose the exact problem with any confidence. After several days in the hospital and countless prayers from my young parents, my father went to the hospital chapel one night; things were desperate. He got down on his knees and prayed to God. He again asked God to heal me, and he surrendered me to God for whatever God wanted. The next day, the problem mysteriously disappeared. I was soon released to go home. God had healed me.

Nothing is too hard for the Lord. Is this not the repeated teaching of the Bible?

> *Ah, Lord God! It is you who have made the heavens and the earth by your great power and by your outstretched arm! Nothing is too hard for you.*
> —Jeremiah 32:17

> *The word of the Lord came to Jeremiah: "Behold, I am the Lord, the God of all flesh. Is anything too hard for me?"*
> —Jeremiah 32:26–27

> *For nothing will be impossible with God!"*
> —Luke 1:37

> *But Jesus looked at them as said, "With man this is impossible, but with God all things are possible."*
> —Matthew 19:26

> *Now to him who is able to do far more abundantly than all that we ask or think, according to the power at work within us, to him be glory in the church and in Christ Jesus throughout all generations, forever and ever. Amen.*
> —Ephesians 3:20–21

Is this not the way God works throughout the Bible, doing the miraculous and the impossible? Is this not the nature of God himself and part of the very "Godness" of God? The living God is a miracle-working God!

According to Martin Luther in his *Large Catechism:*

> We always ask for less than we should and don't even think God is willing to give us what we ask for. We don't ask the right way. We don't understand that what we pray about is more important than we can comprehend. We think small, but the Lord is great and powerful. He expects us to ask for great things. He wants to give them to us to demonstrate his almighty power.[1]

What are you facing today, right now, that seems impossible? Perhaps, like Abraham and Sarah, you have been waiting so long. Does your problem seem impossible? Revisit the unforgettable words of Genesis 18:14. Write those words on your heart.

God's message to Sarah is God's message to you: *"Is anything too hard for the LORD?"*

Chapter 2

AS CLOSE AS WE GET

*Suppose there are fifty righteous within the city.
Will you then sweep away the place and not spare it for the
fifty righteous who are in it?*
—Genesis 18:24

I was riding in a car in China with Andy Hamilton, who had been a classmate in seminary. At one point Andy said, "Intercession is as close as we get to the cross." He meant that when we pray for someone, it is an act of sacrificial love, best seen in the cross of Christ. Intercession is largely unseen and hidden. It takes time and energy. It is hard work. It costs us. As one pastor said: "Intercession is a sacrifice. A bleeding sacrifice."

But we intercede because we care about the people we pray for. It's as close as we get to the cross. Intercession is not just a sacrifice. It is also a privilege. In fact, it is the highest ministry we can have. It is the best and most loving thing we can do for someone because we are bringing that person to God and accessing the power of God on their behalf. It is not the *only* thing we can do for someone, but it is the *best* thing we can do for someone.

The more intercession in a church, the healthier the church, the healthier the individuals in the church, and the more answers to prayer in the church. A spirit of intercession is vital for a healthy church. Dietrich Bonhoeffer, the German pastor, wrote: "A Christian fellowship lives and exists by the intercession of its members for one another, or it collapses."[2]

In Genesis 18:16–33, God lets Abraham know that he is about to judge the city of Sodom because he wants Abraham to intercede for his nephew Lot who lives in that city. God says to Abraham:

> *Because the outcry against Sodom and Gomorrah is great and their sin is very grave, I will go down to see whether they have done altogether according to the outcry that has come to me. And if not, I will know.*
>
> —Genesis 18:20–21

God is testing Abraham to see whether Abraham cares enough about Lot to intercede for him—to *fervently* intercede for him. Will Abraham care enough about Lot and Lot's family to intercede with all his heart? Will Abraham intercede for Lot even though it is a sacrificial, selfless act of love?

Just as God wanted Abraham to pray for Lot, so God wants us to pray for the people in our lives.

God will burden us with certain people, certain needs, and certain hurts because he wants us to pray for them. He wants us to intercede for them. He wants us to care.

God has called you to intercede because you are God's friend, just like Abraham was God's friend. You are God's partner, God's ally. You have clout with God. This is our duty and our privilege. Who is it that God is putting on your heart to regularly intercede for, with passionate and persistent prayer? Ask God who it should be. Be sensitive to whoever God is placing on your heart.

First, praying for someone shows love. Second, it shows that we understand God's heart for people, and third, it shows faith. It demonstrates that we trust God to work in response to our prayer.

Earlier we saw that God was prompting Abraham to pray for Lot. Abraham responds to this prompt and begins to intercede:

> *Will you indeed sweep away the righteous with the wicked? Suppose there are fifty righteous within the city. Will you then sweep away the place and not spare it for the fifty righteous who are in it? Far be it from you to do such a thing, to put the righteous to death with the wicked, so that the righteous fare as the wicked! Far be that from you! Shall not the Judge of all the earth do what is just?*
> —Genesis 18:23–25

We are immediately struck by how honest Abraham is in this prayer—how bold he is, how emotional he is. Abraham is not holding back. He is deeply stirred by the possibility that God might wipe out the city of Sodom, where his nephew Lot and

Lot's family live. Abraham *cares!* Abraham cares, so he prays. He prays with passion, with fervor, with emotion, with honesty.

He's thinking: "God, how could you wipe out this city? How could you wipe out an entire city if there are righteous people living in the city? God, what if there are fifty righteous people living in the city? Will you spare it for the sake of those fifty? Far be it from you, O God, the Judge of all the earth, to sweep away the righteous with the wicked. Far be it from you!"

God loves our honesty in prayer. We see it all through the Bible—with Moses, with David, with Jeremiah, with Job, and with Jesus. God loves it when we are real and authentic in prayer. God can handle our honesty. He knows how we are feeling, and he would much rather that we talk with him honestly and openly than withdraw into a sullen and angry silence.

God gives no indication that he is in any way displeased with Abraham's boldness and honesty. So Abraham keeps asking:

> *Behold, I have undertaken to speak to the Lord, I who am but dust and ashes. Suppose five of the fifty righteous are lacking. Will you destroy the whole city for lack of five? And he said, "I will not destroy it if I find forty-five there."*
> —Genesis 18:27–28

Abraham approaches God, not with arrogance, but with humility. However, he is bold; he is bold with his persistent prayer. Because he cares about Lot, he does not shrink back from coming to God with boldness. He believes that God is approachable.

In the same way, God wants us to be bold in asking for things, whether for ourselves or for other people. He wants us to know that he is approachable, that he listens. Hebrews 4:16 calls us to boldness in prayer: *"Let us then with confidence draw near to the throne of grace, that we may receive mercy and find grace to help in time of need."* God wants us not only to intercede, but to intercede with bold persistence—to pray and keep on praying.

Abraham continues to press the case with God. Abraham asks about fifty people. "Yes!" Then he asks about forty-five people. "Yes!" Then he asks about forty people. "Yes!" Then he asks about thirty people. "Yes!" Then he asks about twenty people. "Yes!" Then he asks about ten people. "Yes!"

"Yes! Yes! Yes!" Of course this does not mean that God always says yes to our requests. However, he might well say yes, and so we ought to ask and keep on asking. In Luke 18:1 we read of Jesus: *"And he told them a parable to the effect that they ought always to pray and not lose heart."*

Every time we ask God for something, it shows faith. It shows that we believe that God is God, that God hears prayer, that God cares, that God has the power to intervene. To some extent, every time you pray, you express faith in God. So we must pray and keep on praying.

It surprises me that Abraham stops at ten people, rather than four people, which would include the four people in Lot's family. But notice what happens. In Genesis 19, God destroys the city of Sodom. But before he destroys the city, God sent angels to force Lot and his immediate family to leave the city. This was God's response to Abraham's intercession. Then we read in Genesis 19:29: *"So it was that, when God destroyed the cities of the valley, God remembered Abraham and sent Lot out of the midst of the overthrow when he overthrew the cities in which Lot had lived."*

God remembered Abraham. God heard Abraham's prayer for Lot. Actually, Abraham never mentioned Lot in his prayers, but God knew Abraham's heart. He knew what Abraham was asking: protection for Lot and his family. God answered the prayer of Abraham's heart.

God is teaching us what he was teaching Abraham. He was teaching Abraham that prayer is the most powerful thing we can do for someone. He was teaching Abraham that prayer is the real work. Prayer is the greater work. Prayer is the most powerful work. Yes, there are mysteries about prayer that we do not understand. That is no surprise since God is the incomprehensible God, and we cannot put him in a tidy, theological box. However, over and over again, in the Bible, God tells us: "Ask! Ask! Ask!" And so we ask.

Prayer is where the power is. As Charles Spurgeon put it, "Prayer is the slender nerve that moves omnipotence."[3] In fact, the real power in the world belongs not to the politicians, not to the wealthy, not to the business elite, but to the intercessors.

Abraham had clout with God because he was God's friend. God wanted Abraham to intercede. In the same way, if we know Christ as our Savior, then we are God's child. We are God's friend, and we have clout with God. God wants us to intercede. God has given us the high privilege of intercession, bringing people before the throne of God and asking God to intervene.

Do you know the story of D. E. Hoste, who succeeded Hudson Taylor as the leader of the China Inland Mission? Early in his ministry, Hoste was working with two villages in China. In the village where Hoste lived, people were not thriving spiritually. But the people in the other village across the mountain range were doing great. From time to time he visited them, and they were always thriving. So he began to ask God what was going on. How could those believers across the mountain range be doing better than the believers with whom he lived and worked? [4]

The Lord showed him the answer. Although he was spending much time counseling, preaching, and teaching those with whom he lived, he spent much more time in prayer for the other village. Hoste concluded that there were four basic elements in making disciples: (1) prayer, (2) prayer, (3) prayer, and (4) the Word—in that order and in about that amount.

The power of intercession: it's as close as we get to the cross.

CHAPTER 3

NOT DESPERATE ENOUGH

I will not let you go unless you bless me.
—Genesis 32:26

The best way to learn about prayer is to study the prayers in the Bible. In Genesis 32, the patriarch Jacob, Abraham's grandson, prays a rather startling prayer: *"I will not let you go unless you bless me."* God had taken human form and wrestled with Jacob. Jacob was saying that he would not let go of God physically unless God blessed him.

This prayer ranks as one of the unique prayers in all the Bible, and it comes in one of the most bizarre episodes in all the Bible. This is the story. Jacob has lived his life relying upon his own wits. He has made his way by scheming and manipulating. Over the years in a foreign land, he has accumulated considerable wealth, and now he is returning to his homeland with the foreboding prospect of meeting his brother, Esau. Twice Jacob had wronged Esau. By this time, Esau has amassed a large following of servants and workers. He could easily destroy Jacob and his family. Jacob was terrified, and the normally self-reliant Jacob finally recognizes his need for God. Jacob felt helpless.

On the night before Jacob encounters Esau, a stranger attacks Jacob in the darkness. They begin to wrestle, and they continue wrestling through the night. The wrestling match was exhausting for Jacob. During the long night of wrestling, it gradually dawns on Jacob that this stranger is none other than God himself—God in human form.

When God is ready to depart, Jacob holds on for dear life. He won't let go of God. Clinging to God, he pleads, *"I will not let you go unless you bless me!"*

For the first time in his life, Jacob comes to the point where he is desperate for the blessing of God. He wants the blessing of God. He needs the blessing of God. This is new for Jacob. At this vulnerable time, just before his dreaded encounter with Esau, he can no longer rely on his own wits and scheming. Jacob is desperate . . . for God.

Jacob pleads for God's blessing. In fact, the prophet Hosea will later write of Jacob wrestling with God: *"He wept and sought his favor"* (Hosea 12:4).

What is going on in Jacob's prayer? The prayer sounds a bit selfish, but God clearly loved this prayer and answered it. Indeed, God would bless Jacob richly, beyond his wildest dreams.

The prayer reflected not selfishness but helplessness. The prayer reflected his dependence upon God, which is the foundation of all true prayer. Jacob, who epitomized the self-reliant schemer, is finally dependent upon God not himself. It's as if Jacob is saying, "Lord, I need you! I need your grace. I need your protection. I need your blessing. Without your blessing, my brother will annihilate me and all that I have. Lord, I'm not letting go of you unless you bless me."

This is desperate prayer. This is helplessness. This sense of dependence is the foundation of biblical faith, and therefore, it is the foundation of biblical prayer.

Norwegian pastor Ole Hallesby settled on the single word *helplessness* as the best summary of the heart attitude that God accepts as prayer: "Whether it takes the form of words or not does not mean anything to God, only to us. Only he who is helpless can truly pray."[5]

By contrast, the great enemy of prayer is self-reliance. At times, we all struggle with the tendency to rely upon ourselves and our own resources. It begins when we are toddlers, insisting, "I can do it myself." That may be humorous in a two-year-old, but it is not so humorous when we grow up to become proud, independent adults. Self-reliant adults never give voice to it, but this is their mindset: "I can do it myself. In fact, I am the only one I can really trust. Everyone else will let me down . . . including God."

I have had all kinds of struggles in marriage, parenting, pastoring, health, mental disease, ministry disappointments and failures—all kinds of struggles, some of which seemed overwhelming. I do *not know* why God brought these trials or allowed them. But this is what I *do know*: Each of our trials deepens our sense of helplessness, brokenness, and weakness before God. God uses pain and suffering to show us how much we need him.

Jackson Senyonga, a pastor in Uganda who lived through genocide under Idi Amin and the revival that came later, once spoke to a group of Christians in Houston. Sarona Rameka quotes Senyonga as saying: "You in America are not desperate enough."[6]

Each of us must ask ourselves this question: To what extent does self-reliance characterize me? Perhaps more than we recognize. Do we go through life depending on our own devices, our own resources, our own efforts? Or do we have such a sense of helplessness before God that prayer is our first response and our only hope?

What a story we find in Genesis 32—the night Jacob wrestled with God. What is God saying to us through this passage? "Give up your sinful self-reliance and depend upon me. Give up all your scheming, deception, and manipulation. Call out to me. Surrender yourself deeply to me. Recognize that your weakness is an opportunity for my strength. Learn to trust, completely and continually in my blessing, my favor, my protection."

George Verwer, the founder of the worldwide ministry Operation Mobilization, wrote: "The lack of prayer is the greatest scandal in the church today. It is a greater scandal than the disunity, the immorality, the lack of love."[7]

Theologian Peter T. Forsyth expressed the same thought:

> The worst sin is prayerlessness. Overt sin . . . or the glaring inconsistencies which often surprise us in Christian people are the effect of this, or its punishment. . . . Not to want to pray, then, is the sin behind sin.[8]

Chapter 4

SHOW ME YOUR GLORY

Please show me your glory.
Exodus 33:18

Every morning when I meet with God for prayer and Bible reading, I come to a time of intercession. Invariably, my first request reflects Moses's prayer in Exodus 33:18: *"Lord, show me your glory."*

However, in my case I make the request plural: "Lord, show us your glory." The *us* refers to my immediate family—my wife Gayle, our three kids and their spouses, our nine grandchildren (so far!), and for me. I begin with this prayer from Exodus 33 because in some ways, I look at this request as *the* most foundational prayer request. If we see God in his glory, if we grasp his greatness and his goodness, then everything else in the spiritual life falls into place.

For decades I have regarded the slim volume by A. W. Tozer, *The Knowledge of the Holy,* as one of my favorite books. Tozer begins the book with this unforgettable sentence: "What comes into our minds when we think about God is the most important thing about us."[9] Tozer gets it exactly right. If we see God as he is, then we will respond to God as we ought—with love, trust, obedience, and worship.

In many ways this is what I am asking when I pray: "Lord, show us your glory." I am asking God to show us who he really is, in all his beauty and majesty. Each morning when I pray this prayer, "Lord, show us your glory," I invariably elaborate it. I continue: "Show us your love, your power, your greatness, your goodness."

This audacious prayer of Moses is so striking, both in its context and in God's response. Since the beginning of the book of Exodus, Moses has seen the greatness of God. He has seen God's power and glory in the burning bush, in the ten plagues, in the splitting of the Red Sea and the destruction of Pharaoh's army, in the pillar of fire that led the Israelites, and much more. Perhaps more than any other book in the Old Testament, the book of Exodus reveals the glory of God, the majesty of God, the grandeur of God, the power of God, the sovereignty of God, the holiness of God.

Yet, after all that Moses has seen, he wants still more of God. So he makes this bold request in Exodus 33:18: *"Please show me your glory!"* This prayer reflects Moses's enormous passion for God. This is not a passion for what God can do for Moses, but a passion for God himself. This is a passion, not for God's hand, but for God's face. Not for God's gifts, but for God himself.

We see this same passion for God in the theologian Augustine, when he wrote:

> Give me a man in love; he knows what I mean. Give me one who yearns; give me one who is hungry; give me one far away in this desert, who is thirsty and sighs for the spring of the Eternal Country. Give me that sort of man; he knows what I mean. But if I speak to a cold man, he just doesn't know what I am talking about. [10]

Augustine's prayer reflects the same passion for God that we see in Moses in Exodus 33.

What did God think of Moses's prayer? Apparently, God loved this prayer because he responded positively to this request: *I will make all my goodness pass before you and will proclaim before you my name 'The LORD'"* (Exodus 33:19).

It is fascinating that when God reveals his glory to Moses, the focus is not upon his greatness but upon his goodness. God says, *"I will make all my goodness pass before you."* Of course, we know that God's greatness is vital to his glory, but the glory of God was primarily reflected to Moses by the goodness of God.

The next morning, God does what he promised and revealed his glory to Moses:

> *The Lord descended in the cloud and stood with him there, and proclaimed the name of the Lord. The Lord passed before him and proclaimed, "The Lord, the Lord, a God merciful and gracious, slow to anger, and abounding in steadfast love and faithfulness, keeping*

steadfast love for thousands, forgiving iniquity and transgression and sin, but who will by no means clear the guilty, visiting the iniquity of the fathers on the children and the children's children, to the third and the fourth generation."

—Exodus 34:5–7

And how does Moses respond to this overwhelming revelation of the glory of God? *"And Moses quickly bowed his head toward the earth and worshiped"* (Exodus 34:8). How else could he respond?

Jonathan Edwards is commonly regarded as the greatest theologian in American history. He was a towering intellect, but oh, he had such passion for God himself. He described his encounter with God:

> Once . . . *anno* 1737 . . . [in] divine contemplation and prayer, I had a view that for me was extraordinary, of the glory of the Son of God, as Mediator between God and man, and his wonderful, great, full, pure and sweet grace and love, and meek and gentle condescension. . . . The person of Christ appeared ineffably excellent with an excellency great enough to swallow up all thought and conception . . . which continued as near as I can judge, about an hour; which kept me the greater part of the time in a flood of tears, and weeping aloud. I felt an ardency of soul to be, what I know not otherwise how to express, emptied

and annihilated; to lie in the dust, and to be full of Christ alone; to love him with a holy and pure love; to trust in him; to live upon him; to serve and follow him; and to be perfectly sanctified and made pure, with a divine and heavenly purity.[11]

This is a Moses-like encounter with the glory of God. The prayer of Moses in Exodus 33 is not simply an audacious request, but is a foundational request. How vital it is that we see God and experience God in his glory. This is a prayer for us to pray. "Lord, show me your glory. Lord, show us your glory."

Chapter 5

LISTENING PRAYER

Speak, for your servant is listening.
—1 Samuel 3:10 NIV

The classic passage on listening prayer in the Bible is found in 1 Samuel 3 when God speaks to the boy Samuel. The first verse of the chapter is telling: *"Now the boy Samuel was ministering to the Lord in the presence of Eli. And the word of the Lord was rare in those days; there was no frequent vision."* The clear implication is that the Word of the Lord is not always rare. The voice of God is not always infrequent. This was an exceptional time because of the grievous sin of the people. Normally, it was not uncommon for God to speak.

The story unfolds in 1 Samuel 3:2–14 (NIV):

> *One night Eli, whose eyes were becoming so weak that he could barely see, was lying down in his usual place. The lamp of God had not yet gone out, and Samuel was lying down in the house of the* Lord, *where the ark of God was.*
>
> *Then the* Lord *called Samuel. Samuel answered, "Here I am." And he ran to Eli and said, "Here I am; you called me." But Eli said, "I did not call; go back and lie down." So he went and lay down.*
>
> *Again the* Lord *called, "Samuel!" And Samuel got up and went to Eli and said, "Here I am; you called me." "My son," Eli said, "I did not call; go back and lie down." Now Samuel did not yet know the* Lord*: The word of the* Lord *had not yet been revealed to him.*
>
> *A third time the* Lord *called, "Samuel!" And Samuel got up and went to Eli and said, "Here I am; you called me." Then Eli realized that the* Lord *was calling the boy. So Eli told Samuel, "Go and lie down, and if he calls you, say, 'Speak,* Lord*, for your servant is listening.'" So Samuel went and lay down in his place.*
>
> *The* Lord *came and stood there, calling as at the other times, "Samuel! Samuel!" Then Samuel said, "Speak, for your servant is listening."*
>
> *And the* Lord *said to Samuel: "See, I am about to do something in Israel that will make the ears of everyone who hears about it tingle. At that time I will*

> *carry out against Eli everything I spoke against his family—from beginning to end. For I told him that I would judge his family forever because of the sin he knew about; his sons blasphemed God, and he failed to restrain them. Therefore I swore to the house of Eli, 'The guilt of Eli's house will never be atoned for by sacrifice or offering.'"*

God would continue to speak to Samuel for the rest of his life. No doubt Samuel got more words from God than the typical Israelite because he was the leading prophet in the land. But did God speak to others? What we find throughout the Bible, from Genesis to Revelation, is that God speaks to his people.

He spoke to Adam and Eve. He spoke to Noah. He frequently gave Abraham special promises and leadings. Jacob had a dream. Moses got a burning bush and numerous revelations and leadings. Joseph, Deborah, Samuel, the parents of Samson, Elijah, David (so many times), Solomon, and Daniel—all heard from God. As did the major and minor prophets of the Old Testament, Peter, Paul, Philip, Agabus, and on and on.

The Bible is full of occasions when God speaks to his people with impressions, leadings, dreams, visions, even an audible voice at times. God speaks! And not just to apostles and prophets. For example, in Acts 9 God gives a vision with clear revelation to a disciple named Ananias. All through the Bible, God speaks to his people.

Here is the issue: Is the Bible a book of exceptions or is the Bible a book of examples. The prayer of Samuel is a prayer for each one of us: *"Speak, Lord, for your servant is listening."*

Unfortunately, for most of us, the mindset is *not "Speak, Lord, for your servant is listening,"* but "Listen, Lord, for your servant is speaking."

If we are going to take the Bible as our guide, and not just the tradition we grew up in or the opinion of some teacher, then we must conclude: This is the way God deals with his people. This is the way God has always dealt with his people. He speaks, and he speaks to us in all kinds of ways. Certainly, God speaks in Scripture, but he also speaks with impressions, leadings, convictions, dreams, and visions. The living God is the God who speaks.

It is theoretically possible that the Bible is full of God speaking to his people in all kinds of ways, from Genesis to Revelation, and yet this is not the way God deals with us today. It is possible that the Bible is a book of exceptions. But it is extremely unlikely. The Bible itself makes it clear that it is a book of examples not a book of exceptions, a book written for our instruction and guidance.

Yes, the Bible is unique. It is God's authoritative written Word, and it stands as judge and arbiter over all else. But if we follow the Bible, and not simply give lip service to the Bible while we actually follow the traditions of man, then we will take the biblical view that God speaks to his people in all kinds of ways. Yes, everything must be evaluated by Scripture, but God speaks to us in many ways.

Down deep, we know that God speaks. If he is anything, he is a God who speaks, a God who reveals, a personal and loving God. We don't follow a philosophy or a religion or a book of dry theology. We have a personal, love relationship with God. Of course God speaks into our lives and leads us.

The problem is that we all have seen listening prayer abused. We have heard some believer state, "God told me such and such," and we were quite sure that God had *not* told them that. But just because a gift can be abused does not mean that there is no legitimate use of that gift. We use our discernment, just as God tells us to. But we must not quench the Spirit. This is the simple instruction of the Apostle Paul in 1 Thessalonians 5:19: *"Do not quench the Spirit."*

Listening prayer demands a large dose of humility. Rather than pronounce, "God told me," as if we were an Old Testament prophet, perhaps we should say, "I think God said to me."

One challenge with hearing from God is our lack of silence and solitude. Most of us have far too much noise in our lives and in our heads. We seem to have an aversion to quietness and stillness. Blaise Pascal wrote: "All of man's misery is derived from his inability to sit quietly by himself in a room alone."[12]

If we fill our lives with noise, words, and activity, it will be difficult for us to hear the voice of God. David Brainerd, who was close to the great Puritan theologian Jonathan Edwards, wrote:

> In the silences I make in the midst of the turmoil of life I have appointments with God. From these silences I come forth with spirit refreshed, and with a renewed sense of power. I hear a voice in the silences and become increasingly aware that it is the voice of God.[13]

There are churches and organizations which insist that listening prayer is not biblical. But they are inconsistent in. For instance, they believe that God convicts us of sin. That's God speaking. They believe we can pray Psalm 139:23–24:

> *Search me, O God, and know my heart!*
> *Try me and know my thoughts!*
> *And see if there be any grievous way in me,*
> *and lead me in the way everlasting!*

They believe God calls us to leave one job and go to another job. That's God speaking. Where does the Bible say that God speaks with conviction of sin or with calling but not in other ways? If we are going to take the biblical view, then we must believe that God speaks to us, not only through Scripture, but in other ways as well.

In fact, God is always speaking to us, and we must be attentive to his voice at all times. Frederick Faber wrote:

> There is hardly ever a complete silence in our soul. God is whispering to us well-nigh incessantly. Whenever the sounds of the world die out in the soul, or sink low, then we hear these whisperings of God. He is always whispering to us, only we do not always hear, because of the noise, hurry, and distraction which life causes as it rushes on.[14]

I want to hear the voice of God better. I need to hear the voice of God better. Samuel's prayer is my prayer: "Speak, Lord, for your servant is listening."

Chapter 6

LEARNING TO HEAR GOD BETTER

Therefore David inquired of the Lord.
—1 Samuel 23:2

There are challenges and difficulties with listening prayer. You may be thinking, "How do we know it is God's voice that I'm hearing and not just my own voice? Some talk so confidently of hearing God, but it is never so clear for me. Often, I ask God to speak with me, and it seems I hear nothing, at least nothing that is clearly of God."

These are good questions. Honest questions. And you will get no simplistic answers from me. I wrestle with these questions also. How can we be biblical with listening prayer?

First, we need to believe that God speaks. Believe the Bible. Then we might ask him to speak to us and to block out all other voices except his voice. And then we must trust that he will put things on our hearts and in our minds.

Silence is important. *"Be still, and know that I am God. I will be exalted among the nations, I will be exalted in the earth"* (Psalm 46:10)! *"For God alone my soul waits in silence"* (Psalm 62:1). And it's not just quietness in the room that we need; we also need quietness in our head.

Be willing to obey the Lord. David would ask God to speak to him:

> *Therefore David inquired of the Lord, "Shall I go and attack these Philistines?" And the Lord said to David, "Go and attack the Philistines and save Keilah." But David's men said to him, "Behold, we are afraid here in Judah; how much more then if we go to Keilah against the armies of the Philistines?" Then David inquired of the Lord again. And the Lord answered him, "Arise, go down to Keilah, for I will give the Philistines into your hand." And David and his men went to Keilah and fought with the Philistines and brought away their livestock and struck them with a great blow. So David saved the inhabitants of Keilah.*
>
> —1 Samuel 23:2–5

David obeyed the Lord. If David had stopped obeying, then God would have stopped speaking to him. We too must inquire of the Lord: "Lord what should I do about this problem?" And we too must be ready to obey.

Also, be aware of any barriers to hearing God. Sin will separate us from God and block the voice of God in our lives. Perhaps you don't *want* to hear God's voice because you're afraid of what he might say. Maybe you feel unworthy of hearing God. Perhaps you are not willing to stop talking long enough to hear God! Be aware of barriers to the voice of God.

It's important that we don't demand God to speak. He is not our servant. *We* are the servants. The main thing is just to be in God's presence and enjoy his loving presence, whether or not we hear something from God. We ask of God, not demand of God.

In *The Chronicles of Narnia*, Aslan says of Uncle Andrew:

> "He thinks great folly, child," said Aslan. "This world is bursting with life for these few days because the song with which I called it into life still hangs in the air and rumbles in the ground. It will not be so for long. But I cannot tell that to this old sinner, and I cannot comfort him either; he has made himself unable to hear my voice. If I spoke to him, he would hear only growling and roarings. Oh Adam's sons, how cleverly you defend yourselves against all that might do you good! But I will give him the only gift he is still able to receive."[15]

Do not make yourself *unable* to hear the voice of God. Gordon MacDonald tells this anecdote:

> At lunch a couple of weeks back, a man I greatly respect (age 60 this month) responds to my question, "What's God been saying to you since we

were last together?" He says, "I've spent my whole life running, achieving. You know me—I've been a hammer, and everyone else has been the anvil. I've tried to fill every moment with something to do. I've always been telling God what I wanted . . . what I thought He should be doing. But now I'm learning that praying is as much about listening and waiting as all my previous talking. And each time I've listened, and each time I've waited, God has done something —small or large—that has left me breathless and aware of how much I've missed in all my busyness."[16]

Beware of the busyness that blocks the voice of God. Along these lines, A. W. Tozer gives strong testimony of how powerful listening prayer can be:

> When I am praying the most eloquently, I am getting the least accomplished in my prayer life. But when I stop getting eloquent and give God less theology and shut up and just gaze upward and wait for God to speak to my heart he speaks with such power that I have to grab a pencil and a notebook and take notes on what God is saying to my heart.[17]

Oswald Chambers, the author of *My Utmost for His Highest*, gives this valuable advice: "Get into the habit of saying, 'Speak, Lord,' and life will become a romance . . . one great romance, a glorious opportunity for seeing marvelous things all the time."[18]

I'm not that good at listening prayer, but it is sweet to be silent before the Lord, to be open to what he puts on your heart and in your mind, to ask him a question, and then be still and listen. It is one thing to hear a message from a Christian friend, but it is a much deeper thing to hear a message from God, for God to speak deeply into your soul about his love for you, about what you should focus on.

Most days, I ask the Lord something like this, "Is there anything that I need to hear from you today?" Then I will be quiet, in both voice and mind, and perhaps I will sense an impression like this from the Lord: "Jeff, this ministry event is not about you. It is all about Jesus." Or "Jeff, today you just need to focus on loving me and enjoying me." These may not seem like profound or life-changing messages, but they are heart-changing when they come from the Father.

If listening prayer is not a regular part of your prayer life, what should you do? Here are two prayers that resonate with my soul. The first is from Richard Foster, in his superb book on prayer:

> My Lord and my God, listening is hard for me. I do not exactly mean hard, for I understand that this is a matter of receiving rather than trying. What I mean is that I am so action oriented, so product driven, that doing is easier for me than being. I need your help if I am to be still and listen. I would like to try. I would like to learn how to sink down into the light of your presence until I can become comfortable in that posture. Help me to try now. Thank you. Amen.[19]

The second prayer comes from A. W. Tozer:

> Lord, teach me to listen. The times are noisy and my ears are weary with the thousand raucous sounds which continuously assault them. . . . let me hear you speaking in my heart. Let me get used to the sound of your voice, that its tones may be familiar when the sounds of earth die away and the only sound will be the music of your speaking voice. Amen.[20]

Michael Mickan is a close friend who has coached me in listening prayer. In one of our meetings, he shared these suggestions:

> Admit right from the start that you are not in control and you are surrendering any desire for that to him. It's God's prerogative when and how he chooses to speak, so listening isn't so much about what God says as your attitude of waiting for him like a faithful servant, ready to obey what his master says.
>
> Ask the Holy Spirit repeatedly to guide you. Admit that you'll mess it up if you try to do this right and that you entrust yourself to the Holy Spirit's lead. God will speak in all kinds of ways and at different times, and just asking the Holy Spirit to guide you in listening is crucial so that you don't focus on some "posture" or performance-oriented method. Again, this is about an attitude of listening rather than method designed to elicit a response from the Lord.

Quiet your mind. We can be still on the outside and busy on the inside. Quiet your mind and just *be* before the Lord. Focus on him. Take a posture of quiet waiting for the Lord.

Be ready to respond if the Lord says something to you. If you already have decided what you will and will not do before you listen, what's the point of listening?

While you're going through your time with God, or preparing your sermon, or doing anything throughout the day, repeatedly stop yourself and ask, "Lord, is there anything you want to say about this?" Then actually wait to see if the Lord has anything to say. In time, I doubt you will have to mentally go through this exercise; you'll most likely just *be* in this attitude, which is what you're aiming for.

Hold on to what you *hear* lightly. Be prepared to *hear* wrongly. Between our brokenness, spiritual interference, and the condition of sin in this world, you won't always hear correctly. Sometimes, it's just what you might be saying to yourself. Be ready to trash whatever you thought you heard if it doesn't turn out. Your willingness to move forward even in the face of your error is an act of submission. It's why I never say, "The Lord said . . ." but always say something to the effect of, "I believe the Lord might be saying . . ." or "I think the Lord might be leading that . . ." It's not a lack of confidence, just a recognition of brokenness.

Chapter 7

HEART ON FIRE

Yours, O Lord, is the greatness and the power and the glory and the victory and the majesty, for all that is in the heavens and in the earth is yours. Yours is the kingdom, O Lord, and you are exalted as head above all.
—1 Chronicles 29:11

The climactic event in the life of King David—one of the milestone events in all the Old Testament—is found in 1 Chronicles 29.

David has come to the end of his forty-year reign as king over Israel. In fact, he is at the end of his life, and he will soon turn over the kingdom to his son Solomon. So David gathers the leaders of the people together for a final convocation. He tells them how he has given generously to build the temple. Then the leaders respond by giving generously and joyfully. Everyone is so excited about this great celebration. Finally, Israel will have a temple for God in Jerusalem and not just the tabernacle.

At this point of high emotional fervor, David lifts his voice in prayer before all the people. He praises God for his unspeakable greatness, power, glory, majesty, and splendor. This prayer ranks as one of the most magnificent prayers in all the Bible:

> *Therefore David blessed the LORD in the presence of all the assembly. And David said: "Blessed are you, O LORD, the God of Israel our father, forever and ever.*
>
> *Yours, O LORD, is the greatness and the power and the glory and the victory and the majesty, for all that is in the heavens and in the earth is yours. Yours is the kingdom, O LORD, and you are exalted as head above all. Both riches and honor come from you, and you rule over all. In your hand are power and might, and in your hand it is to make great and to give strength to all. And now we thank you, our God, and praise your glorious name."*
> —1 Chronicles 29:10–13

Do you sense the heart of David? The passion of David? The depth of his emotion? David is completely overwhelmed and undone by the greatness and the glory of God. He lacks the words to fully express all that is on his heart.

If David was anything, he was a worshipper. His heart is bursting with love, praise, and wonder. David exuded such an exalted view of God. David had this burning heart for God, a heart lost in love and adoration. And here at this solemn moment, he cannot hold back his heart. He cannot *not* worship. He erupts in this sublime outburst of heartfelt praise.

This is what worshippers do. They have seen the glory of God. They have tasted the goodness of God. They have felt the love of God. And . . . They . . . Worship. With all their hearts, they worship. Worshippers have seen the glory of God, and their hearts are set on fire.

Dear friend, this is the God we pray to. We do not pray to a tame, safe, and small God. We pray to the God who is unfathomably great, glorious, holy, and majestic. Our God is the King of the universe, and he rules over all things everywhere.

When you begin your prayer with praise like this, it changes everything. You are reminded of just who it is that you are talking with. You are reminded that God is bigger than the entire universe, and he is certainly bigger than your biggest problem. You are encouraged that whatever your need is, God can take care of it. You begin to see your problems from a heaven-bound perspective rather than from an earth-bound perspective.

To begin your prayers by praising God is the *right* thing to do. It is right because God is so great and because he is worthy of our praise. But to begin your prayers with praise is also the *wise* thing to do because we need to be reminded of who God is. We need to right-size our problems. We need God's perspective on our challenges.

When I was a new Christian and a freshman at Rice University, nearly fifty-two years ago, I memorized 1 Chronicles 29:11. For over fifty years, this sublime outburst of praise has been implanted in my mind and on my heart. Over the decades I have gone back to this verse time after time after time. Sometimes, I pray this verse in my daily prayer time with the Lord. Sometimes, I pray it with our church in a worship service or prayer service. This is one of the great verses in the Bible on the glory of God. Implant this verse in your heart.

David pours out his soul with adoration and deep worship. Because God is the sovereign God of the galaxies, he has all greatness, power, glory, victory, and majesty in the universe. Because God is sovereign, David exclaims: *"For all that is in the heavens and in the earth is yours."* David is saying: "God, you own it all. It all belongs to you. You made the world, you rule the world, you sustain the world. Everything in the heavens and everything in the earth belongs to you."

David continues: *"Yours is the kingdom, O LORD, and you are exalted as head above all."* He is saying, "God, you rule the universe as the sovereign God over all. You are exalted as the King and Head of the universe." David could hardly give more emphasis to the sovereignty of God.

When we come to God the way David came to God, when we see God the way David saw God, when we know that God is the sovereign, infinite God of all glory and honor, then it is impossible for prayer to be boring. It is impossible to have drab thoughts of God. Rather, we grab our crash helmets because we come into the presence of the Almighty.

David was overcome with the greatness and the glory of God. He was undone. Because he was a worshipper.

Friend, do you know what this feels like? Do you know what it is to be overcome with the greatness and the glory of God? When we see God in his greatness and in his goodness, we cannot *not* worship.

Do you see God the way David saw God? Are you one of those people with a heart on fire?

Chapter 8

A PLEA FOR PRAYER

If my people who are called by my name humble themselves, and pray and seek my face and turn from their wicked ways, then I will hear from heaven and will forgive their sin and heal their land.
—2 Chronicles 7:14

J. Edwin Orr, a scholar on revival, related the following events:

> After the Revolutionary War in America, our country was in serious moral decline. Drunkenness was epidemic. Out of a population of only 15 million people, there were 300,000 confirmed drunks, with 15,000 of them dying monthly. Profanity was at shocking levels. Women were afraid to go out alone at night for the first time in our country's history. Bank robberies were a daily occurrence.

All the churches were in decline. The largest denomination, the Methodists, were losing more members than they were gaining. The second largest denomination, the Baptists, were in their most wintry season ever. The Episcopalians, the Congregationalists, and the Lutherans were all languishing.

Chief Justice John Marshall said that Christianity was too far gone to ever be rescued. In France, Voltaire said that Christianity would be forgotten in 30 years, and Thomas Paine gleefully spread this message across our country.

During this time, a search was done at Harvard and not one believer was found. Princeton was supposed to be a better place, but only two believers were found there. At one college they held a mock communion. At another college they burned a Bible in public. At some schools there were so few Christians that they had to meet in secret. It seemed to many people that Christianity might not survive in America.

What did God do about this desperate situation? In 1794 a pastor by the name of Isaac Bachus wrote a pamphlet called "A Plea for Prayer." The pamphlet was widely read in our country.

Networks of people began meeting on Mondays for prayer. The prayer movement spread across the states. It was not long before revival broke out in Connecticut. Then it spread to Massachusetts. Eventually it would reach even the frontier region.

Kentucky was especially known as a place of ungodliness and lawlessness, but in 1800 revival broke out in that region. It spread to Tennessee, then to North Carolina and South Carolina, and to other states. The spiritual landscape of the country began to change.

In the aftermath of this revival, there came a worldwide missions movement. People began calling for the abolition of slavery. Colleges were founded all over the country by revivalists. The United States was transformed.[21]

Who can doubt that we need a similar work of God in our country today? Is our country not also full of depravity, iniquity, and perversity of every kind? There is widespread divorce, the breakdown of the family, alcoholism, opioids, abortion, human trafficking, all kinds of drug abuse, pornography, racial injustice, crime, greed, sexual immorality, child abuse, sexual abuse, and much more. The spiritual and moral climate in our country continues to spiral downward.

Who can doubt that we are in desperate need of revival? We do not simply need improved legislation, better government, lower inflation, judicial reform, and improved schools. *We need a spiritual revival.*

Furthermore, the biggest problem in our country is *not* the failure of unbelievers. No one expects lost people to walk with God. The biggest failure in our country is the failure of the church to be the church. It has been said, "The tragedy of the hour is that the situation is desperate, but the people are not." A. W. Tozer wrote:

> Our most pressing obligation today is to do all in our power to obtain a revival that will result in a reformed, revitalized, purified church. It is of far greater importance that we have better Christians than that we have more of them.[22]

In light of the desperate situation in our land, do we not need to give fresh attention to the poignant words of 2 Chronicles 7:13–14?

> *When I shut up the heavens so that there is no rain, or command the locust to devour the land, or send pestilence among my people, if my people who are called by my name humble themselves, and pray and seek my face and turn from their wicked ways, then I will hear from heaven and will forgive their sin and heal their land.*

In this poignant passage there are four essential elements for revival. First: *"If my people who are called by my name humble themselves."* If we are going to see a movement of God in our midst, it will begin with humility. It will begin with brokenness, contrition, and repentance. Psalm 51:17 says, *"A broken and contrite heart, O God, you will not despise."* If we want the favor and blessing of God, then we must humble ourselves before Almighty God. We must decide that God is God, and we are not. We must decide that it is Jesus, and not us, who is the point of the story. We must decide to lie low and exalt Christ alone.

Second: *"If my people who are called by my name humble themselves, and pray."* Dr. A. T. Pierson said: "There has never been a spiritual awakening in any country or locality that did not begin with united prayer."[23] Prayer is part of humbling ourselves. It is the first part. Because in prayer, we admit our desperate dependence upon God. We admit our helplessness before God.

Have you come to the place where you recognize that there will never be a significant breakthrough in your life apart from prayer? Have you realized that we will never experience spiritual transformation in our country apart from prayer? Not just a little prayer. Or occasional prayer. Or mechanical prayer. But frequent prayer. Fervent prayer. United prayer. Sustained prayer.

God uses people who pray. God uses churches that pray. As Charles Spurgeon said, "Whenever God wants to do a great work, he first sets his people to pray."[24]

Dr. Orr also related the events in New York City in the 1850s:

> The city was prosperous, and people felt little need to call upon God. But then a financial crash swept away so much wealth. Thousands of merchants were forced to the wall as banks failed and railroads went into bankruptcy. Factories shut down, and vast numbers of people were thrown into unemployment. New York City alone had 30,000 unemployed men. The hearts of people were thoroughly weaned from financial speculation, while hunger and despair stared people in the face.

On July 1, 1857, a businessman named Jeremiah Lamphier took up an appointment as a city missionary in downtown New York. Burdened by the great need, Lamphier decided to invite others to join him in a noonday prayer meeting, to be held on Wednesdays. He distributed a handbill that said: "A Prayer Meeting is held every Wednesday, from 12 to 1 o'clock, in the Consistory building in the rear of the North Dutch Church, corner of Fulton and William Streets."

Accordingly, at 12 noon, September 23, 1857, the door was opened and the faithful Lamphier took his seat to await the response to his invitation. Five minutes went by, and no one appeared. He paced the room in a conflict of fear and faith. Ten minutes elapsed. Still no one came. Fifteen minutes went by. Lamphier was still alone. Twenty minutes. Twenty-five minutes. Thirty minutes. And then at 12:30 a step was heard on the stairs, and the first person appeared. Then another, and another, and another. Until six people were present and the prayer meeting began. The following Wednesday, October 7, there were 40 intercessors.

Then in the first week of October 1857, it was decided to hold the prayer meeting daily instead of weekly. Within six months, 10,000 businessmen were gathering daily for prayer in New York City. Within two years, a million converts were added to American churches. Undoubtedly the greatest revival in New York's history swept the city, and the whole nation was curious. There was no fanaticism and no hysteria, but only an incredible movement of people to pray.[25]

Third: *"If my people who are called by my name humble themselves, and pray and seek my face."* We do not simply seek God's hand. We seek God's face. We are not just seeking God for the things that he can give us. Of course, we do seek God's hand because we are dependent upon him. We need him! But first, we seek his face. We seek God for himself—for his own sake and not simply for what we need from him. We seek God because we love him, and he is worthy of our worship. We seek his face because we are desperate people.

Fourth: *"If my people who are called by my name humble themselves, and pray and seek my face and turn from their wicked ways."* It is not enough to pray and read the Bible. It is not enough to go to church and serve and give. Revival begins with repentance. With obedience. With turning from our wicked ways.

To quote A. W. Tozer again:

> Have you noticed how much praying for revival has been going on of late—and how little revival has resulted? I believe the problem is that we have been trying to substitute praying for obeying, and it simply will not work. To pray for revival while ignoring the plain precept laid down in Scripture is to waste a lot of words and get nothing for our trouble. Prayer will become effective when we stop using it as a substitute for obedience.[26]

If we truly believe that God is God and we are not, then we will obey him. We will bow our knees to him. We will do what he says. This means that if anything in our lives is more important to us than God—be it money, career, house, hobby, sports, political party, or family—anything at all that is more important to us than God, then it is idolatry. Right now perhaps the Spirit of God is putting something on your heart that you need to surrender afresh to him. If so, do it right now. Your liberation is found in surrender to God. Your freedom is found in obedience.

What happens when we do these four things? God promises, *"Then I will hear from heaven and will forgive their sin and heal their land."* This is the sure promise of God.

If we respond to God in this way, then God gives us this incredible three-fold promise: *"Then I will hear from heaven and will forgive their sin and heal their land."* How we need God to hear our prayers. How we need God to forgive our sin. How we need God to heal our land. We need God to pour out his Spirit upon us in a fresh way. We need spiritual breakthroughs in every area of our lives.

Leonard Ravenhill was asked, "Why is there no revival today?" He replied, "Because the people of God are content without it."[27]

Chapter 9

OUR EYES ARE ON YOU

We do not know what to do, but our eyes are on you.
—2 Chronicles 20:12

One of the classic prayers in the Bible comes from King Jehoshaphat in 2 Chronicles 20. Jehoshaphat receives the terrifying news that a massive army from three nations has gathered to attack Judah.

How does this godly king respond to this heart-shattering crisis? *"Then Jehoshaphat was afraid and set his face to seek the Lord, and proclaimed a fast throughout all Judah"* (2 Chronicles 20:3).

What was his first response? *"He set his face to seek the Lord."* Whenever we encounter a crisis or a problem of any size, our first response must *not* be to fret and worry—though that is a big temptation. Our first response must *not* be to plan and strategize—though we may do that later. Our first response is *not* even to call upon people who can help us—though we might do that later. Our *first* response is to set our face to seek the Lord. Our first response is prayer. Prayer is not a last resort, but a first response. Because prayer is the real work! Prayer is where the power is.

Jehoshaphat also proclaims a fast. At times, God will lead us to a season of prayer and fasting. All through the Bible, at special times of burden and challenge, the people of God fast and pray. They go without food to express their deep dependence upon God, their hunger for God. Just like with prayer, fasting has special power when we fast together as a community. God seems to take special delight when his people fast and pray together. We are saying to God with our actions, "Lord, I am desperate for you!"

What else do we learn about prayer from Jehoshaphat's amazing prayer? Verse 6 of 1 Chronicles 20 says, *"O Lord God of our fathers, are you not God in heaven? You rule over all the kingdoms of the nations. In your hand are power and might, so that none is able to withstand you."*

Jehoshaphat is caught up in the greatness of God, the power of God, the sovereignty of God, the glory of God. Like many other classic prayers in the Bible, such as the prayer of David in 1 Chronicles 29, King Jehoshaphat begins with the greatness of God. His prayer is more God-centered than man-centered.

One reason to begin prayer with praise is simply because God is worthy of all our praise. But another reason to begin with praise is because it puts our problems in perspective. We begin to view our problems from God's perspective rather than from our perspective.

Ultimately, what matters is not the size of our problems, but the size of our God! When we begin with praise, we remind ourselves how big God is. Jehoshaphat has an overwhelming problem—an impossible problem. But God was bigger than his problem because God is the sovereign, infinite, all-powerful God. Begin your prayers with praise.

One challenge with prayer is praying in front of other people because we have a tendency to want to shape our prayers to impress others. The antidote is to remind ourselves that we are standing in the presence of God, and he is our only audience. In verse 9 of 1 Chronicles 20, Jehoshaphat prays, *"If disaster comes upon us, the sword, judgment, or pestilence, or famine, we will stand before this house and before you."* Here is the perspective for public prayer: "Lord, we are standing before you, in your presence."

Then Jehoshaphat says that *"we . . . cry out to you in our affliction."* Note the strong verb: *cry out.* Jehoshaphat is not going through the motions. He does not mouth a bored, lukewarm prayer. No, he cries out to God. And we know that God loves passionate prayer. He loves it when we come to him fervently, earnestly, desperately. It was Charles Spurgeon who said, "Lukewarm prayers ask God not to hear them."[28]

Jehoshaphat continues in prayer:

> *And now behold, the men of Ammon and Moab and Mount Seir, whom you would not let Israel invade when they came from the land of Egypt, and whom they avoided and did not destroy – behold, they reward us by coming to drive us out of your possession, which you have given us to inherit.*
>
> —2 Chronicles 20:10–11

Where did Jehoshaphat learn these things? From Scripture. He had read these things in Scripture, and this infused his prayer. Here we have another learning about prayer. Prayer and the Word go together. Pray as you read the Bible. Read the Bible as you pray. Pray Bible-infused prayers.

In 2 Chronicles 20:12, we come to one of the most compelling prayers in the Bible: *"For we are powerless against this great horde that is coming against us. We do not know what to do, but our eyes are on you."*

This is beautiful. Jehoshaphat is saying, "Lord, we have no power. We have no wisdom. But our eyes are upon you!" This is dependence upon God. Desperateness for God. Humility before God. Trust in God.

All true prayer flows out of dependence upon God. It was Leonard Ravenhill who wrote, "The self-sufficient do not pray, the self-satisfied will not pray, the self-righteous cannot pray."[29]

At this point God pours out his Spirit upon the people and gives a prophetic word through one of the prophets:

> *You will not need to fight in this battle. Stand firm, hold your position, and see the salvation of the Lord on your behalf, O Judah and Jerusalem. Do not be afraid and do not be dismayed. Tomorrow go out against them, and the Lord will be with you.*
>
> —2 Chronicles 20:17

Can you imagine being in the crowd that day, knowing that a vast army is coming against you to annihilate you and your family, and you hear the sure word of the prophet that God will protect you completely? Can you imagine the collective sigh of the people? They just got word from God that their lives would be spared! Can you imagine their eyes welling up with tears, their jaws hanging open? Can you imagine the unrestrained shouting and joy?

In prayer, remember the battle is not yours, but God's. Do not be afraid or dismayed. God says this is his battle. He's got this. Whenever we pray, we must remind ourselves: "The battle belongs to God, not me."

After this life-changing prophecy, how do Jehoshaphat and the people respond?

> *Then Jehoshaphat bowed his head with his face to the ground, and all Judah and the inhabitants of Jerusalem fell down before the Lord, worshipping the Lord. And the Levites, of the Kohathites and the Korahites, stood up to praise the Lord, the God of Israel, with a very loud voice.*
> —2 Chronicles 20:18–19

The only fitting response to God's rescue is worship. Whole-hearted worship. Whole-hearted, whole-bodied worship. Not feeble, mechanical singing, but loud, enthusiastic singing.

One pastor said, "Everything that God says to do in the house of God—raise your hands, clap your hands, dance, shout, cry out—we do in the football stadium."[30] When God rescues us in crisis, is this not worth celebrating?

The touching sequel comes in verse 21:

> *And when he had taken counsel with the people, he appointed those who were to sing to the L*ORD *and praise him in holy attire, as they went before the army, and say, "Give thanks to the L*ORD*, for his steadfast love endures forever."*

Why does Jehoshaphat put the worship leaders in front? Because he took God at his word, that the battle was the Lord's and that he would deliver his people. When the worship leaders went out praising God, then God routs the enemy.

We are reminded of a final prayer principle in this passage. Worship is warfare. Praise is a weapon of war. We live our entire lives in wartime. An epic spiritual battle rages across the galaxies. But when we praise God, the enemy flees. Worship is warfare.

I don't know about you, but I plan to worship and praise God every day of my life. First, because God is worthy of worship. Second, I want God's perspective on my problems, but third, worship is warfare, and I want the enemy to flee.

What a passage . . . what a prayer. So many things to learn about prayer in 2 Chronicles 20. Here are the seven vital principles:

1. Prayer is not our last resort, but our first response. Begin with prayer.
2. There are special times when we should not simply pray, but pray and fast.
3. Begin with praise and the greatness of God. Make your prayers God-centered, not man-centered.

4. Remind yourself in public prayer that you stand in the presence of God, and not just people.
5. Make your prayers passionate, not lukewarm.
6. Infuse your praying with Scripture.
7. Remind yourself that the battle belongs to God, not to you.

Finally, worship is warfare. When we worship, the enemy flees.

Chapter 10

PASSIONATE LOVE

*O God, you are my God,
earnestly I seek you;
my soul thirsts for you;
my flesh faints for you,
as in a dry and weary land
where there is no water.*
—Psalm 63:1

David's passionate love for God is nowhere more pronounced than in Psalm 63. In fact, passion for God may be more emphatic in Psalm 63 than in any in other passage in all the Bible. Listen to David as he pours out his heart to God:

> O God, you are my God; earnestly I seek you;
> my soul thirsts for you;

> *my flesh faints for you,*
>   *as in a dry and weary land where there is no water.*
> *So I have looked upon you in the sanctuary,*
>   *beholding your power and glory.*
> *Because your steadfast love is better than life,*
>   *my lips will praise you.*
> *So I will bless you as long as I live;*
>   *in your name I will lift up my hands.*
> *My soul will be satisfied as with fat and rich food,*
>   *and my mouth will praise you with joyful lips,*
>   —Psalm 63:1–5

Do you hear David's heart for God? His longing for God? Does it move you? Does it awaken something deep in your heart? Augustine understood David's heart. He wrote these words:

> Give me a man in love; he knows what I mean. Give me one who yearns; give me one who is hungry; give me one far away in this desert, who is thirsty and sighs for the spring of the Eternal Country. Give me that sort of man; he knows what I mean. But if I speak to a cold man, he just doesn't know what I am talking about.[31]

Let the words of the psalm sink deeply into your soul.

"O God, you are my God."

In light of the likely historical background of the psalm, David is saying: "My whole world has unraveled. I am fleeing from my own son Absalom, who is out to kill me. Yet, you, O

Lord, are still my God. You are my rock, my strong tower, my fortress. You and you alone are my God."

"Earnestly I seek you."

His prayer is fervent, passionate, wholehearted! He does not pray a tepid, drowsy, lifeless prayer. He's not half-hearted. No, he is seeking God with all his heart. For David, this was not religion or duty. This was love affair. This was sacred romance. *"Earnestly I seek you."* We see this same intensity in Augustine's prayer:

> You flashed, you shone;
>   and you chased away my blindness.
> You became fragrant;
>   and I inhaled and sighed for you.
> I tasted,
>   and now hunger and thirst for you.
> You touched me;
>   and I burned for your embrace.[32]

David continues: *"My soul thirsts for you; my flesh faints for you, as in a dry and weary land where there is no water."* David is in the Judean desert. There is little water. He experiences physical thirst. The painful thirst of dry, parched lips. But his deepest thirst is for God himself. He yearns for God.

In fact, his hunger for God affects his entire body: *"My flesh faints for you."* What passionate love. What burning zeal for God. David did not just want God's gifts, the things that God could give him. David wanted *God himself.*

Then in verse 3, David prays these remarkable words:

> *Because your steadfast love is better than life, my lips will praise you.*

There it is! "Your love, O Lord, is better than life itself. I would rather have you than all the world has to offer." Augustine posed a crucial question: "If God came to you and offered to meet all of your needs, but told you that you would never see his face, how would you respond?"[33]

For David, this would be a no-brainer. David needed God's hand, God's gifts. But even more he hungered for God's face. David exuded passionate love for God himself.

What about you? Have you tasted the rich, embracing love of God? Have you experienced the relentless tenderness and affection of the Lord Jesus Christ? Have you been dazzled, overwhelmed and undone by his grace and by his love?

Mother Teresa was going through a dry period in her spiritual life, and yet she still had such a passion for Christ that she penned this prayer: "I want to love you Jesus like you have never been loved before."[34]

What a heart for God. Why do some people have such unusual passion for Christ? I don't know. Ultimately, this kind of heart for God is a gift. Every good thing is a gift from God. But you can ask for the gift. "Lord, give me this kind of heart for you, this thirst for you, this love for you!"

Chapter 11

THE LANGUAGE OF LOVE

*Oh sing to the L̲o̲r̲d̲ a new song;
sing to the L̲o̲r̲d̲, all the earth!*
—Psalm 96:1

Singing to God is at once a most powerful expression of prayer and yet a most neglected expression of prayer. At least, in our private prayer lives, it is often neglected. This may not be true for you, but it is for many people.

Some people feel uncomfortable singing to God. Others may not recognize the importance of worshiping God in song. But others may neglect singing to God because they are such bad singers.

But consider several things: You are driving alone in your car listening to music, and you hear a song that completely transforms your mood. Maybe the music makes you somber and reflective, when a moment before, you felt content. Or perhaps a song instantly lifts your mood and energy when you felt fatigued or down.

Most would agree that music can set the tone of a room. Whether it's the music playing as a bride walks down the aisle toward her waiting groom, or the song you choose to give that last bit of effort in a workout, or the song you sing at the top of your lungs on a road trip with your best friends. The power of music is undeniable.

Or consider with me how big music is in our culture. Think about how important music is to a movie. It sets the whole tone of the scene. Or consider the untold billions of dollars spent each year on music and music technology.

Music is so pervasive in our culture, so powerful in our daily lives. If that is true for music in general, how much more powerful is music when it is used for its highest purpose—to worship our God in heaven? God created music as an instrument for us to praise him. When we use music for this purpose, we experience more deeply the presence of God. Our daily time with God becomes so much richer.

Singing is a prominent form of praise throughout the Bible, but nowhere is singing more prominent than in the book of Psalms. The very word *psalms* means *songs*. These are the songs of Israel, meant to be sung to God. We have the lyrics but not the music.

In the book of Psalms there are over a hundred references to the word *sing* or the word *song*. For example:

> *But let all who take refuge in you rejoice,*
> *Let them ever sing for joy.*
>
> —Psalm 5:11

I will *sing* praise to your name, O Most High.
—Psalm 9:2

Sing praises to the Lord, O you his saints.
—Psalm 30:4

But I will *sing* of your strength;
I will *sing* aloud of your steadfast love in the morning.
—Psalm 59:16

Oh *sing* to the Lord a new *song*;
Sing to the Lord, all the earth!
Sing to the Lord, bless his name;
Tell of his salvation from day to day.
—Psalm 96:1–2

Oh *sing* to the Lord a new *song*,
For he has done marvelous things!
—Psalm 98:1

Serve the Lord with gladness!
Come into his presence with *singing!*
—Psalm 100:2

And just think, this is only a small sample of the references to the word *sing* or the word *song*. There are so many more verses calling us to sing praises to our God.

Why does our singing matter so much to God? What else can so deeply express what's on our hearts? What else allows us to express so powerfully our love for Jesus?

God created us to sing—even those of us who cannot sing a note! To be more accurate, God created us to sing to *him*. He has implanted a "singing gene" into our souls. This "singing gene" is not the *ability* to sing, but the *desire* to sing to God. It involves our heart not our voice.

We yearn to sing to God. You may have suppressed this yearning, but it is there. There is no need to deprive yourself any longer of this exhilarating pleasure when you connect with God in such a deeply intimate way.

All of this is true for us, both in our private singing, in our time alone with God, and in our public singing, with our community of faith.

Sometimes, when we are singing to God as a church family, there is something about the combination of words, music, praise band, singers, and heartfelt voices that is inexpressibly moving to me, to the point that the beauty and joy is almost painful. But this is the pain of deep joy. The atmosphere is electric, charged with the glory and grandeur of God. It is powerful. The presence of God is so strong in the room that it is nearly tangible.

What is it about singing to God that touches our hearts so deeply? I am not sure. There is a mystery to music that transcends logic. It is a mystery born in the heart of God, who is the Creator of music and the Master Musician.

The godly Jim Elliot, who would eventually give his life for Christ in the Amazon jungle, wrote in his prayer journal about singing:

> Enjoyed the truth of singing "psalms and hymns and spiritual songs" this morning. Found my

> prayer list so unstimulating to real prayer that I laid it aside and took the Inter-Varsity Hymnal and sang aloud with much heart-warming such songs as seemed to fit my need. This is as decidedly a means of grace as anything given by God to His people, but how little we use it![35]

Singing to God is poignant. It's emotional. It's passionate. Singing to God is the language of love.

At times, in our worship, whether privately or publicly, we feel so deeply that only singing can express what we feel inside. Just *saying* the words won't do. We've got to sing them! Augustine said that when we sing, we pray twice—once with words and once at another level in the music of the heart.

Singing is a gift—a gift from God. For when you sing to God, your whole view of God is transformed and elevated, and your heart is moved to love him more.

So sing those songs. Those God songs. Those God songs of love, praise, and wonder. Sing with all your heart . . . sing to God!

Chapter 12

O Begin!

He got down on his knees three times a day and prayed and gave thanks before his God, as he had done previously.
—Daniel 6:10

The most significant words in this verse come in the final clause: *"as he had done previously."* This was Daniel's everyday practice—his way of life. Every day, three times a day, he would go to his rooms at set times. He would get down on his knees. Then he would call out to God before the open windows facing toward Jerusalem.

His enemies, jealous of his position with the king, knew that this was Daniel's daily discipline. They knew that if Daniel was alive and breathing, then he would not fail to get on his knees and pray, three times a day, because this was an expression of Daniel's loyalty to his God. This was an expression of Daniel's worship and love for God.

So, these enemies tricked the vain King Darius into passing a law that no one could pray to anyone except the king for thirty days, on penalty of being cast into a den of lions.

When the law was passed, Daniel was undeterred. Apparently, he did not even have to think about this matter, even though it was a life-and-death issue. Because of his devotion to God, he continued to do what he did every day. He met with God—unhurried time alone with God. This is what Daniel did every day to seek his God, and he would do it no matter if it meant death. It was simply a matter of loyalty to God.

So much could be said about this passage on the priority and the urgency of meeting with God. But we also see one practical principle for prayer: Get a daily plan to meet with God and stick to that plan. Be steadfast with this plan no matter what. Find a place where you can pray and meet with God. Set a time that works for you. Get a reading plan for Scripture each day. Over time, shape the plan to fit your spiritual thumbprint.

God nowhere commands us to do exactly what Daniel did. But biblical priorities, biblical examples, and historical examples all suggest that we carve out a special time every day to meet alone with God for prayer and Bible reading. This is a time to prize. A time to prioritize. A time to protect.

Yes, we want to pray throughout the day—an ongoing conversation with our Father. But it is wise to have a special time with God each day. Maybe it's not a long time but it is *your* time. It is *your* time to talk and listen and get alone with God, no matter what else happens during your day. This is your time to connect with God. During this time, God will restore your soul and prepare you for whatever the day brings.

One of the greatest verses in all Scripture is found in Matthew 11:28 where Jesus says, *"Come to me, all who labor and are heavy laden, and I will give you rest."* Certainly this applies to non-Christians coming to Jesus for salvation. It also applies to Christians in times of crisis or special burden. But it also applies to us every day. Every day we have burdens and problems, and we need to come to Jesus. We bring our burdens and our weariness to him, and we receive his peace and his rest.

Down through history, men and women of God have set aside a special time to meet with the Lord. Like Daniel, they developed a plan to meet with God and followed it. This was their delight, not their duty.

Hudson Taylor was one of the greatest missionaries in Christian history. He led the way to open the interior of China to the gospel, and he had incredible impact around the world. *Hudson Taylor's Spiritual Secret*, written by Hudson's son Howard and his wife, is one of my all-time favorite biographies. Howard describes making a trip across northern China with his father in which they would stop each night at an inn for travelers, and all the guests would sleep in one big open room.

Every night at two in the morning, Hudson Taylor would turn on his lantern. Then he would get out his New Testament and spend two hours with the Lord, from two to four o'clock, so that he would not be interrupted in that crowded room with all those travelers. Like Daniel, Hudson Taylor had a set time and a set place for his daily meeting with God.

At the end of Hudson Taylor's life, it was said of him: "For forty years the sun never rose on China that God didn't find him on his knees."[36] Again, this was not legalism or duty; it was privilege and delight.

John Wesley, the founder of the Methodist Church and one of the most influential Christian leaders in history, once spoke to his followers about this daily time with God:

> O begin! Fix some part of every day for private exercises. Whether you like it or not, read and pray daily. It is for your life; there is no other way: else you will be a trifler all your days.[37]

I find this to be such a challenging quote. A trifler is someone who is just messing around. This is the person who is not serious or devoted to a cause. Unless we fix a set time and place to meet with God daily, then it is quite likely that we will be triflers all our days. Triflers with God.

If you "fix some part of every day for private exercises," it will not be confining for you, but liberating. This discipline is not a matter of legalism but a matter of heart and desire.

When I was a young man in my twenties, I ran marathons professionally. I would train about 100 miles per week, and six days a week, I worked out morning and afternoon. On Sunday, an easier day, I would only run once. During that season of my life, I would never wake up and ask myself: Should I run today or not? I had already made that decision. Every day I would go out and run unless I was very sick. There was great freedom in having pre-decided that I would run.

Just to have an example, this is what my daily time with God looks like. I wake up early and drive about five minutes to my office. It is still dark outside, and I am the only one on campus when I arrive. I make a cup of coffee. Then I begin to slowly walk in the darkened hallways of our staff building, meeting with the Lord. I begin with a time of singing, worshipping, and praying. This is a time of praise, worship, and thanksgiving when I bask in God's love and presence. During this time I normally include a brief period of quietness before the Lord, asking him, "Lord, is there anything that I need to hear from you today?" I journal some about the previous day.

After that, for the next hour I read, meditate, and pray in Scripture, picking up with the passages where I stopped the previous day, one in the Old Testament and one in the New Testament. However far I get in that hour, I mark my place and begin at that verse the next day.

After this time of worship and Bible reading, I move on to a time of intercession for the people God has put on my heart—family, close friends, coworkers, people in our church, lost friends, and others. For this time of intercession, I normally drive to a nearby forest trail. For four gentle miles, alone with God in the forest, I run and intercede for the people God has placed in my life.

This is my typical pattern during this season of my life. But my time with God is forever evolving. I simply wanted to relate one detailed example to spur your thinking. But here is the bigger point: I never wake up and decide whether I should meet with God that day. That question has already been decided. To pre-decide is so liberating.

Friend, if you are serious about knowing Jesus Christ, then resolve to meet with God every day. Get a plan, find a place, set a time. Enjoy the privilege of life, drawing close to God.

Hear again the wise words of Wesley: "O begin! Fix some part of every day for private exercises. Whether you like it or not, read and pray daily. It is for your life; there is no other way: else you will be a trifler all your days."[38]

Chapter 13

DANIEL'S CLASSIC PRAYER

O my God, incline your ear and hear. Open your eyes and see our desolations, and the city that is called by your name. For we do not present our pleas before you because of our righteousness, but because of your great mercy.
—Daniel 9:18

Because prayer is absolutely vital to the spiritual life, we want to become the best "pray-ers" we can be. As I mentioned in chapter 3, one of the best ways to learn about prayer is to eavesdrop on the great prayers in the Bible. One of the classic biblical prayers is found in Daniel 9.

The passage begins with Daniel understanding from the Scriptures that the desolation of Jerusalem would last seventy years. This realization evoked a deep prayer response in Daniel. There is so much in this prayer, but five things loom large.

First, Daniel's prayer is deeply rooted in Scripture. In verse 2 of chapter 9, we read: *"I, Daniel, perceived in the books the number of years that, according to the word of the Lord to Jeremiah the prophet, must pass before the end of the desolations of Jerusalem, namely, seventy years."*

This great prayer in Daniel 9 begins in Scripture. It is Scripture-prompted prayer, Scripture-based prayer. Regularly soaking in the words of the Bible provides fuel for our prayer life.

Several other references to Scripture are included in this prayer. For example, Daniel 9:13 says, *"As it is written in the Law of Moses, all this calamity has come upon us."* Daniel is probably not reading his Bible at the time, but he had filled his mind with God's Word, and this in turn propelled his praying. Our prayer must be deeply rooted in Scripture. Prayer and Scripture go together.

Second, Daniel's prayer has striking fervency. In Daniel 9:3 we read: *"Then I turned my face to the Lord God, seeking him by prayer and pleas for mercy with fasting and sackcloth and ashes."* Daniel pleaded with God. He poured his heart into the prayer. This was not a polite, lukewarm, mechanical prayer. No, this is full-out, fervent, passionate, whole-hearted, agonizing prayer.

There is deep emotion all through this prayer. Daniel did not "say his prayers." Daniel prayed. He cried out to God. He poured out his heart to God. We see this fervor throughout the prayer. Verse 19 is another example: *"O Lord, hear; O Lord, forgive. O Lord, pay attention and act. Delay not, for your own sake, O my God, because your city and your people are called by your name."*

I do not say that every prayer has this much fervor. But sometimes, our prayer should be white-hot with passion. And all our prayer must come straight from the heart.

Third, Daniel's prayer reveals a lofty view of God. This principle invariably applies to the classic prayers in the Bible. People with an exalted view of God, who see God as sovereign, infinite, immortal, eternal, holy, magnificent and all-powerful, cannot help but become people of prayer. Their prayers are powerful because they see God in his greatness.

If we have a dull and drab prayer life, maybe it's because we have a dull and drab view of God, and we need to see God as he truly is—the way Daniel saw him. These are examples in this kind of prayer:

> Daniel 9:4. *"O Lord, the great and awesome God, who keeps covenant and steadfast love with those who love him and keep his commandments."*
>
> Daniel 9:7. *"To you, O Lord, belongs righteousness."*
>
> Daniel 9:9. *"To the Lord our God belong mercy and forgiveness, for we have rebelled against him."*
>
> Daniel 9:14. *"Therefore the L*ORD *has kept ready the calamity and has brought it upon us, for the L*ORD *our God is righteous in all the works that he has done, and we have not obeyed his voice."*

This principle is critical. The more we see God as he is, as the great and holy God who is our Father and who is crazy in love with us, the more God-pleasing our prayers become. Our prayer life reveals how we actually see God. How we view God is revealed, not in our statements *about* God, but in the way we speak *to* God in prayer.

Fourth, Daniel's prayer is marked by profound brokenness. The entire prayer oozes brokenness, contrition, and confession.

Keep in mind that Daniel is one of the godliest men in all the Bible. In fact, we do not see one sin or weakness of Daniel's in the entire book. Of course, Daniel was not sinless, but he walked so closely with God. Yet, in this prayer, he does not simply confess the sins of other people. He confesses his own sins. He never says: "They have sinned!" Rather, he always says, *"We have sinned."*

Daniel's spirit of brokenness is found throughout the prayer. For example, in Daniel 9:5–6, he prays:

> ***We*** *have sinned and done wrong and acted wickedly and rebelled, turning aside from your commandments and rules.* ***We*** *have not listened to your servants the prophets, who spoke in your name to our kings, our princes, and our fathers, and to all the people of the land.* (emphasis added)

Similarly, in Daniel 9:11, he says, *"And the curse and oath that are written in the Law of Moses the servant of God have been poured out upon* ***us****, because* ***we*** *have sinned against him."* (emphasis added)

This is true of the entire prayer; it is always, *"We have sinned"* and never "They have sinned." Daniel exudes deep humility and brokenness. No doubt God loved Daniel's brokenness because the Bible teaches that God draws close to those who are broken and contrite in spirit.

Fifth, Daniel's ultimate concern is the glory of God. This is so important. Daniel is not primarily concerned with the people of Israel or with his own comfort and desires, but with the glory of God—with God's reputation and name. Daniel's prayer is God-centered, not man-centered. It is certainly not self-centered.

For example, in Daniel 9:17, he prays: *"Now therefore, O our God, listen to the prayer of your servant and to his pleas for mercy, and for your own sake, O Lord, make your face to shine upon your sanctuary, which is desolate."* Notice that he says, *"For your own sake."* His concern is for God's reputation and glory.

Again, in Daniel 9:19, he prays, *"O Lord, hear; O Lord, forgive. O Lord, pay attention and act. Delay not, for your own sake, O my God, because your city and your people are called by your name."* Notice that Daniel pleads with God to act for *"your own sake"* . . . because your people are called by *"your name."* God is the point of Daniel's prayer. It's all about God: "Lord, you will be honored if you deliver your people."

In 1540 Luther's good friend, Frederick Myconius, became deathly sick and expected to die in a short time. One night he wrote, with trembling hand, a fond farewell to Luther, whom he loved very much. When Luther received the letter, he immediately sent back the following reply:

> I command you in the name of God to live because I still have need of you in the work of reforming the church. The Lord will never let me hear that you are dead, but will permit you to survive me. For this I am praying, this is my will, and may my will be done, because I seek only to glorify the Name of God.[39]

Myconius had already lost the faculty of speech when Luther's letter came—yet in a short time, he was well again. And, true enough, he survived Luther by two months.

Nothing makes us so bold in prayer as when we can look into the eyes of God and say to him: "You know that I am not praying for personal advantage, nor to avoid hardship, nor that my own will in any way should be done, but only for this, that your Name might be glorified."

This is the real test of whether you are a true intercessor: Are you so caught up in God's glory, name, and reputation that your prayer is God-centered. This is not a technique. It is something that comes from within, from deep in your heart, when your whole life is devoted to loving God and knowing God. Then, your prayer naturally becomes God-centered.

Chapter 14

NEVER FORGET

Our Father in heaven.
—Matthew 6:9

Of all the prayers in the Bible, there is none greater than the Lord's Prayer. This is not only the most famous prayer in the Bible, but it is also the most profound prayer in the Bible. At the same time, it is one of the simplest prayers in the Bible. What Leon Morris said of John's Prologue (John 1:1–18) is also true of the Lord's Prayer. It is "deep enough for a whale to swim in and shallow enough for a child to wade in."[40] The Lord's Prayer is both profound and simple.

If the best way to learn how to pray is to study the prayers in Scripture, then the best prayer of all to study is this one. We know this prayer as the "Lord's Prayer," but perhaps it would be more accurate to call it the "Disciples' Prayer." After all, this is one prayer that Jesus could *not* pray, with its confession of sin. It is also the prayer where Jesus is explicitly teaching his disciples how to pray. In fact, he prefaces the prayer with these words: *"Pray then like this"* (John 6:9).

Jesus is *not* so much telling us to say these words, though that is certainly a good thing. Rather, he is teaching us to pray in this way, with this heart, with this perspective. The prayer has a simple structure. Opening address to God, six requests, and closing doxology:

Opening address to God:	"Our Father in heaven."
Six requests:	God's name. God's kingdom. God's will. Give us. Forgive us. Deliver us.
Closing doxology:	"For your is the kingdom and the power and glory forever. Amen."

Both the opening address and the closing prayer are God-centered prayers. Then there are six requests, with the first three focused on God and the last three focused on us.

The first thing to note in the prayer is how Jesus addresses God. Keep in mind that Jesus is teaching his disciples, and us, how to pray. In this model prayer, he addresses God as *"Our Father in heaven."* This term of address has both affection and majesty. God is our Father (affection), and God is in heaven (majesty). At once we see both the goodness and the greatness of God, twin truths that we find throughout Scripture.

When Jesus referred to God as "Our Father," that would have startled his first-century audience of Jews because the

Jews never called God *"Father"* and neither did anyone else. The New Testament scholar Michael Green observed, "You can search Islam and you will not find the name of Father among the ninety-nine names of God. You will search Hinduism or Confucianism in vain. This is unique."[41]

The Hebrew term *"Abba"* is a tender, affectionate, loving name for a father. It is somewhat akin to our term *"Daddy"* or *"Papa."* In many ways, the basic name for God in the New Testament is Father. But many people have had a painful experience with their earthly father. Perhaps your father was an absent father or an alcoholic father or even an abusive father.

If you had a good father, wise and loving, then you understand God as Father by way of comparison. But if you had a bad father, selfish and unkind, then you understand God as Father by way of contrast. After all, no one has had a perfect father on earth, so to some degree all of us understand God as Father by way of contrast. But each one of us can grasp the concept of a good father.

What is the perfect Father like? He is wise, loving, kind, and gentle. He is strong, powerful, fair, and forgiving. He protects us, and he provides for us. He is *good* in every way.

But God is not merely our Father. He is our Father *in heaven*. Heaven is not God's postal address or location, for he fills the universe. The point is that God is not an earthly father, but the Heavenly Father. He is glorious, majestic, exalted, and all-powerful. He is the sovereign, infinite, immutable, and incomprehensible God. He is great beyond all understanding. He is *not* a small God but the eternal I am. He is the God who created the universe by his mere word. He is the God who can hear eight billion people praying at once, no problem. He is the God in heaven.

In one brief title, Jesus has managed to underscore these two critical truths about God: God is good, and God is great. God is our Father, the perfect Father, and therefore he is *good*. He is also our Father in heaven, the exalted and transcendent Father, and therefore he is *great*.

It could well be that the key to prayer is found right here. The most important prayer principle of all is this: Never forget who you are talking with. When you remember *who* you are talking with, who you are praying to—that you are in conversation with the sovereign God of the universe who is also your loving Papa, then it changes everything about prayer. When you consider that the one you come to in prayer is your Father, and he is your Father in heaven—that he is both good and great—it transforms your prayer. Your prayer becomes alive with the glory and grace of God.

Perhaps one reason why some people consider prayer to be boring is because they forget who God is. If you forever keep in mind that God is our loving Father and that he is the infinite God, then it will be impossible to have a boring prayer life. Prayer will become rich and vibrant.

So every time you pray, remind yourself just who it is that you are talking with. He is Father. He is in heaven. He is good, and he is great.

Chapter 15

GOD-CENTERED PRAYER

Hallowed be your name.
—Matthew 6:9

The Lord's Prayer contains six succinct requests. The first three concern God's glory; the last three concern our need.

The first request is *"Hallowed be your name."* The point of this request is, "Lord, may your name be honored, exalted, glorified. Lord, may you get the honor due your holy name." The heart behind this prayer is a blazing passion for the glory of God. Our complete concern must be God's name, not our name; God's reputation, not our reputation; God's honor, not our honor.

The second request is, *"Your kingdom come."* God's kingdom is God's rule in the lives of people. It is not a kingdom over land or territory, but a kingdom over people. We cannot sincerely pray *"Your kingdom come"* unless we mean by this prayer: "May your kingdom come in my life. Take charge of my life. Lord, I surrender to you." This second request is a prayer of surrender.

The third request is, *"Your will be done, on earth as it is in heaven."* This prayer request reminds us of Jesus's prayer in Gethsemane when he prays, *"My Father, if it be possible, let this cup pass from me; nevertheless, not as I will, but as you will"* (Matthew 26:39). This is the prayer of a fully devoted follower of Jesus: "Lord, may your will be done in my life."

Prayer is not about getting what we want from God. It is not trying to get God to change his mind. Rather, prayer is aligning our will with God's will, because God is the sovereign and holy God, and he knows what's best. Prayer is getting on board with what God is doing and surrendering all that we are to a loving Father. Biblical prayer focuses on God's plans, God's desires, and God's agenda, not our plans, our desires, our agendas.

The first half of the Lord's Prayer is strikingly God-centered. It focuses on God's name, God's kingdom, God's will. And then, after three requests for our needs, there is a final God-centered cry: *"For Yours is the kingdom and the power and the glory, forever. Amen"* (Matthew 6:13 NKJV).

Jesus is showing us how to pray. He is showing us to make our prayers God-centered, not self-centered. Focus on God, not yourself. It is not wrong to bring your needs to God. In fact, asking things for yourself expresses a deep humility and dependence on the Lord. However, put the focus of the prayer on the glory and grandeur of God, not on your needs and problems. If we begin our prayer with worship to God, with singing to God, with thanksgiving to God, with surrender to God, then it shifts our gaze off ourselves and onto God. It gives us perspective and right-sizes our problems because we are reminded that however big our problem is, God is bigger.

My daily time with God usually begins with thirty to forty-five minutes of worship. During this time, I normally include these elements:

- I begin this time with praise, which includes singing to God. Often, I will sing a couple of songs to the Lord, perhaps with the help of music on my smartphone.
- Then I might cite one of the great praise passages in the Bible, such as 1 Chronicles 29:11: *"Yours, O Lord, is the greatness and the power and the glory and the victory and the majesty, for all that is in the heavens and in the earth is yours. Yours is the kingdom, O Lord, and you are exalted as head above all."*

    Or I might cite Exodus 34:6–8: *"The Lord passed before him and proclaimed, 'The Lord, the Lord, a God merciful and gracious, slow to anger, and abounding in steadfast love and faithfulness, keeping steadfast love for thousands, forgiving iniquity and transgression and sin, but who will by no means clear the guilty, visiting the iniquity of the fathers on the children and the children's children, to the third and the fourth generation.' And Moses quickly bowed his head toward the earth and worshiped."*

- I always spend some time praising God for his attributes. For example, I often pray: "Lord, I worship you as the sovereign, holy, infinite, eternal, triune, and perfect God. Lord, you are the incomparable and incomprehensible God. God, I worship you because you are perfect in love, grace, mercy, and kindness. You are faithful and forgiving. You are wise and you are just."

In addition to praising God for who he is, I will also take some time in thanksgiving for what God has done. I thank God for his sovereign grace that saved me. I thank him for healing me, both from some serious and mysterious malady when I was four years old and for the substantial healing he has brought to me from obsessive-compulsive disorder as an adult. I thank God for my wife Gayle, our six children (our three biological children and their spouses). I also thank him for our nine grandchildren, our church, for the gifts and calling that God has given me, and more.

Also, during this time of praise, I will normally be quiet before the Lord and listen. If God puts something on my heart, I will jot it down in my prayer journal.

It is not that I pull out a checklist and go through these elements, but this is generally how I begin each day with God. First, I have a sweet time of praise, worship, and thanksgiving. I do not get to petition and intercession until I have taken unhurried time in praise and worship. Then I will take unhurried time praying in Scripture. Only after these two things will I bring my requests and burdens to the Lord.

Each of us has to find our own thumbprint for prayer, but let's make sure that we are following the pattern of prayer found in the Lord's Prayer, making our prayers God-centered rather than man-centered.

Chapter 16

THE HEART OF A FATHER

Give us this day our daily bread.
—Matthew 6:11

In the last two chapters, we looked at two vital principles about prayer taught by Jesus in the Lord's Prayer:

- First, remember who it is you are talking with—the God who is good and the God who is great.
- Second, make your prayers God-centered, not self-centered.

Now, we will give our attention to the third critical principle in the Lord's Prayer: Bring all your needs to God. This third principle gives balance to the second principle. On the one hand, we focus our prayers on God's glory, not on our need. On the other hand, it is imperative that we bring all our needs to God because the very act of making these requests to God expresses dependence, not selfishness.

Let me review the outline of the Lord's Prayer because it is so instructive:

- God-centered Address
- Six Requests:
    1. God's Name
    2. God's Kingdom
    3. God's Will
    4. Give Us
    5. Forgive Us
    6. Deliver Us
- God-centered Doxology

This prayer is so God-centered. First, there is the God-centered opening followed by six requests, the first three of which are God-centered. Then finally, there is the God-centered doxology.

However, Jesus does teach us to bring our own needs and burdens to the Father. In Richard Foster's insightful book *Prayer,* he raises the question of why we should ask God for things when he already knows our needs. Foster explains: "The most straightforward answer to this question is simply that God likes to be asked. We like our children to ask us for things that we already know they need because the very asking enhances and deepens the relationship."[42]

P. T. Forsyth notes, "Love loves to be told what it knows already. . . . It wants to be asked for what it longs to give." [43]

In the Lord's Prayer, Jesus is clearly teaching us to bring our needs to God. When we do that, we are not expressing self-centeredness, but dependence and trust. We are expressing childlike trust. We are saying, "Papa, I need you. Please help me."

Pastor H. B. Charles, Jr. reminds us: "The things you pray about are the things you trust God to handle. The things you neglect to pray about are the things you trust you can handle on your own."[44]

Every time we ask God for something, it inherently glorifies God. With every petition, we implicitly declare:

- "I am not adequate on my own. I need your help."
- "I believe you are God, and I need you."
- "Father, I believe you are good, and you are powerful, and you can rescue me."
- "Lord, help. Lord, rescue. Lord, deliver."
- "I may not have perfect faith, but I have enough faith to come to you and ask."

It is so vital to understand this truth: Every time we ask God for something, it glorifies God. So, do not hold back: Ask! Ask! Ask!

Let's look further at these three model petitions:

- *"Give us this day our daily bread."* This is *provision* for the present.
- *"And forgive us our debts, as we also have forgiven our debtors."* This is *pardon* for the past.
- *"And lead us not into temptation but deliver us from evil."* This is *protection* for the future.

Jesus is teaching us that we can bring all our needs to God, whether present, past, or future; whether physical, spiritual, or relational. We may not get all we want or when we want it or how we want it. God is the sovereign God, not a genie at our beck and call.

Prayer is mysterious and elusive, but this we know: God tells us to ask. In fact, James 4:2 declares: *"You do not have, because you do not ask."* Imagine an enormous warehouse in heaven. (Think of the warehouse in the closing scene of *Raiders of the Lost Ark*.) There are rows and rows of crates, each one with a person's name on it. You go and search for your name. Inside your crate, you find a list of all the blessings God wanted for you, but you never asked for them.

Billy Graham remarked, "Heaven is full of answers to prayers for which no one ever bothered to ask."[45]

From Genesis to Revelation, throughout the entire Bible, God is teaching us: "Ask . . . Ask . . . Ask! I am your Father in heaven." But this principle is especially pronounced in the four Gospels, in the teaching of Jesus. Jesus could hardly be more emphatic that we must ask.

The Lord's Prayer has more, much more to teach us. But this simple, yet epic prayer teaches us three truths about prayer that are absolutely vital to a thriving prayer life:

- Firstly, remember who you are talking with.
- Secondly, make your prayers God-centered, not self-centered.
- Thirdly, bring all your needs to Father, because asking expresses dependence not selfishness.

Chapter 17

ASK!

Ask, and it will be given to you.
—Matthew 7:7

Throughout the Gospels, Jesus teaches us to bring our requests to God. Nowhere is the emphasis more pronounced than in Matthew 7:7–11. In fact, in the first two verses alone, Jesus charges us six times to ask God for things:

> *Ask, and it will be given to you; seek, and you will find; knock, and it will be opened to you. For everyone who asks receives, and the one who seeks finds, and to the one who knocks it will be opened.*
> —Matthew 7:7–8

Jesus could hardly be more emphatic that we must bring our requests to God. Furthermore, Jesus puts equal stress that when we ask, we will receive. This promise has a six-fold reiteration.

Even though Jesus has already given such a strong message on asking and receiving in verses 7–8, he proceeds to make the point three more times in verses, 9–11. This time he does so with colorful imagery:

> *Or which one of you, if his son asks him for bread, will give him a stone? Or if he asks for a fish, will give him a serpent? If you then, who are evil, know how to give good gifts to your children, how much more will your Father who is in heaven give good things to those who ask him!*
> —Matthew 7:9–11

It is as if Jesus is looking deep into our eyes and pleading with us: "Ask! Ask! Ask!"

In his insightful book, *A Praying Life,* Paul Miller writes:

> All of Jesus' teaching on prayer in the gospels can be summarized with one word: *ask.* His greatest concern is that our failure or reluctance to ask keeps us distant from God. But that is not the only reason he tells us to ask anything. God wants to give us good gifts. He loves to give.[46]

Matthew 7:7–11 is also strong on the importance of asking. Despite all these commands to ask and all the promises that we will receive, we cannot help ourselves. We are puzzled; we think: "But I ask for a lot of things that I don't get. How can these passages be true?"

This is a valid question, and there are no simple answers. However, we must consider three truths that help clarify this dilemma.

First, these promises are not made to anybody and everybody. The strong statements in Matthew 7:7–11 come from the Sermon on the Mount. These are promises made to believers who can call God "Father." Furthermore, these are believers who are fully surrendered to Christ, who are poor in spirit, gentle, merciful, hungry and thirsty for righteousness, and much more. They are not perfect people, but they are fully devoted to Christ.

Second, the promise is clarified by the imagery of a child and his father, in verses 9–11. Jesus's point is that God is more ready and willing to give good gifts to his children than we are ready and willing to give good gifts to our children. All loving parents want to give good things to their children, but sometimes, our children ask for things that are not good for them, and for their sake, we say no. If a three-year-old asks for ice cream at breakfast time, the loving parent, knowing best, says no.

If the knowledge gap between us and a three-year-old is so large, we must remember that the knowledge gap between us and God is much larger. After all, the knowledge gap between us and a three-year-old is a finite gap, however large it may be. But the knowledge gap between the smartest adults and God is an *infinite* gap. Our Father in heaven knows best.

For example, when I was young and single, before I met Gayle, I became interested in a young woman as a potential wife. I will call her Rachel. Rachel loved God and had many wonderful traits, and I began hoping that I could marry her one day. I became increasingly infatuated with her and began praying that I could marry her.

But our relationship did not progress. At the time, I was deeply disappointed. Why did God not say yes to my requests? However, years later, I recognized that she was not the right wife for me. She might make a wonderful wife for some other man, but not me. For example, she was too serious and too strict for me. I already struggled with being too serious and too strict. I did not need these traits encouraged. Furthermore, we both struggled with some mental disease. I struggled with OCD, and she struggled with depression. We were not best for each other and God knew that. In his wisdom and in his goodness, God said no to my request.

About a year or so after that relationship ended, I met Gayle. We began dating, and eventually we got married. We have been married for forty-four years. Though I did not realize it at the time, Gayle had the right combination of traits that I needed in a wife. In fact, I consider Gayle the perfect wife for me. God knows what we need so much better than we do.

So far, we have seen two truths that help answer the question about asking for so many things and not receiving them. First, these promises are not made to everyone but to those who are God's children who are fully devoted followers of Christ. Second, God is the perfect Father, and he gives us what is best for us even when we don't realize what that is. He answers not the request we make, but the deeper need behind the request.

But there is a third perspective which we must also keep in mind regarding these commands and promises. Quite often, we ask God for things that he fully intends to give them to us—but not yet. There is waiting involved; the waiting is for our good.

The thing we ask for may be a good thing for us . . . when it is the right time. For it is in the waiting that God so often shapes our souls. It is in the waiting that God teaches us dependence, endurance, gratitude, humility, and faith. God uses waiting to mature us and make us more like Jesus. We may not like waiting, but God uses waiting to shape our souls.

We struggle at times with the mystery of unanswered prayer, but these three clarifications give us perspective. First, remember that the promises are given to those who are fully devoted followers of Christ. Second, God gives us what we truly need, not just what we ask for. Third, God often gives us these things, but not yet.

However, we must not miss the gravity of what Jesus says to us in the Gospels. Jesus is showing us the heart of the Father. This is a Father who loves to be asked. This is a Father who loves to give us what is good. Whenever we ask, God's heart is to say yes.

So ask, ask, ask. And you can know that if this is a good thing for you, at the right time, your loving Father will give it to you. Richard Foster, in his marvelous book entitled *Prayer,* declares:

> The Cambridge professor Herbert Farmer reminds us that "if prayer is the heart of religion, then petition is the heart of prayer." Without Petitionary Prayer we have a truncated prayer life. May I remind us all once again how very much God delights in our asking, looking for an excuse to give.[47]

More succinctly, Augustine wrote, "God is more anxious to bestow his blessings on us than we are to receive them."[48] Friend, look at God. See the heart of a Father, a perfect Father . . . and ask.

Chapter 18

THE SECRET PLACE

And rising very early in the morning while it was still dark,
he departed and went out to a desolate place,
and there he prayed.
—Mark 1:35

Mark 1 records an extremely busy day in the life of Jesus, perhaps his busiest day recorded in the Gospels. He teaches in the synagogue (1:21) where he has a confrontation with a demon and casts a demon out of a man (1:26). He then goes to the home of Peter's mother-in-law where he heals her of a fever (1:31). Perhaps there are other demands placed upon him during the afternoon hours. But in the evening, people start showing up at the door of Peter's mother-in-law, clamoring for Jesus's help. Pretty soon, the whole city has gathered to Jesus, bringing the sick and those oppressed by demons. Jesus heals them all and casts out every demon

(1:32–34). No one was turned away. Quite possibly Jesus spent hours ministering to all the people who wanted his help.

This kind of day exacts a heavy toll—pouring your heart out in teaching, confronting demons, healing scores of people, and having people all around you wanting your time, your help, your attention. Jesus must have been exhausted!

It would be understandable if he took the next day off or at least slept late to recover from the grueling Sabbath day. But what does the next verse tell us? *"And rising very early in the morning, while it was still dark, he departed and went out to a desolate place, and there he prayed"* (Mark 1:35). He rises early. *Very* early. Long before sunrise. He leaves the house and goes to find a secluded place, so he can be alone with his Father—alone in the secret place.

Apparently, this time alone with the Father was so valuable to Jesus, so essential to his spiritual and emotional health, that it was an urgent priority, even after an extremely busy day. God is giving us an indication of what this time in the secret place meant to Jesus—and what it should mean to us.

Then there's Luke's Gospel, which repeatedly underscores the importance of prayer—especially the importance of prayer in the life of Jesus. Prayer is one of the main themes of the book. Here are just some of the examples.

- Luke 5:16 says, *"But he would withdraw to desolate places and pray."* Jesus would regularly withdraw from people to find time in the secret place with the Father. This was Jesus's custom, his practice, just like with the example of Mark 1:35. Luke 5:16 was not atypical, but rather typical of the way Jesus lived his life.

- Luke 6:12. *"In these days he went out to the mountain to pray, and all night he continued in prayer to God."* This was a special occasion. Jesus was about to select his inner group of twelve disciples. And so he prayed *all night.* For Jesus, the urgency of prayer is seen as he spends the entire night in prayer to the Father before this big decision.
- Luke 9:18. *"Now it happened that as he was praying alone, the disciples were with him."* Again, Luke indicates the priority of prayer for Jesus. This is just the way Jesus lived his life. This focus on prayer was normal for him.
- Luke 9:28. *"Now about eight days after these sayings he took with him Peter and John and James and went up on the mountain to pray."* He's getting away from the crowds, away from most of the disciples to talk with the Father. Again, this was the way he lived his life.
- Luke 11:1. *"Now Jesus was praying in a certain place, and when he finished, one of his disciples said to him, 'Lord, teach us to pray, as John taught his disciples.'"* Again, we find Jesus alone with the Father in prayer. This time, one of the disciples asks him, *"Lord, teach us to pray."* We know of no occasion in the Gospels where the disciples asked Jesus to teach them to disciple or preach or heal or cast out demons. But Jesus's praying was so compelling, so powerful, so extraordinary that the disciples could not hold back: *"Lord, teach us to pray!"*
- Luke 18:1. *"And he told them a parable to the effect that they ought always to pray and not lose heart."* Jesus continues to teach the disciples, and us, how to pray. This

time he teaches us to always pray and not grow discouraged if we don't get the answer we want when we want it. Keep on praying! Never give up praying!
- Luke 19:46. *"It is written, 'My house shall be a house of prayer,' but you have made it a den of robbers."* Jesus teaches us that prayer is so vital, so essential, that the essence of the temple is to be a house of prayer. Not a house of teaching. Not a house of biblical scholarship. Not a house of sacrifice. Not a house of worship. But a house of prayer. Prayer was the *sine qua non*.

Prayer was a priority to Jesus, because the Father was a priority to Jesus. Prayer was his main priority. Jesus lived a life of prayer. He was always praying. He was forever going off by himself, to get time with the Father in the secret place. At times, he would even spend hours alone with his Father.

Jesus is showing us how to live life. If prayer was a priority for him, should it not be a priority for us? If it was an urgent matter for him, should it not be an urgent matter for us? If he needed this regular time of prayer, do we not need it? If Jesus longed for this time, should we not long for it? If prayer was essential for him, should it not be essential for us?

One final passage to consider in the life of Jesus is the brief anecdote of Martha and Mary in Luke 10.

> *Now as they went on their way, Jesus entered a village. And a woman named Martha welcomed him into her house. And she had a sister called Mary, who sat at the Lord's feet and listened to his teaching. But Martha*

was distracted with much serving. And she went up to him and said, "Lord, do you not care that my sister has left me to serve alone? Tell her then to help me." But the Lord answered her, "Martha, Martha, you are anxious and troubled about many things, but one thing is necessary. Mary has chosen the good portion, which will not be taken away from her."
—Luke 10:38–42

Can you imagine this scene? Martha is in the kitchen, a blur of frenetic activity to serve Jesus and his disciples. And where's her sister Mary? In the other room. With the men. Sitting at the feet of Jesus. Listening to Jesus.

Finally, Martha's frustration level boils over and she confronts Jesus about her sister Mary not helping. In one sentence she manages to rebuke both Jesus and Mary: *"Lord, do you not care that my sister has left me to serve alone? Tell her then to help me."*

But Jesus, never a pleaser, said no. He essentially tells her, "Martha, one thing is necessary. Mary has chosen the best thing, just being with me, listening to me, seeking me. And no, I won't take that away."

Many Christians are bothered by this passage; they think, "It's not fair. Mary should have been helping Martha." We buy into the American mindset that we must be *doing* something. "Don't just sit there. Do something." But if we are always doing something, then we can easily neglect the inner life, the life of the heart.

There is a time to serve Jesus, to *do* things for Jesus. But there's also a time to simply *be* with Jesus, to seek his face.

In this remarkable passage, Jesus teaches us the priority of just being with him, because we love him and want to love him more. Jesus is looking, not primarily for workers, but for worshippers. Like Martha, we often assume that *doing* for Jesus is more important than *being* with Jesus. There are many people who are workers, *doing* for Jesus. There are far fewer who are worshippers, *being* with Jesus. In Luke 10:38–42, Jesus gives us his perspective about time alone with God, sitting at his feet, seeking his face. This, Jesus says, is the good part, the necessary part. And it won't be taken away.

I don't think for a moment that Jesus looked at his times of prayer as an obligation to perform, a task to complete, a duty to check off. No, time alone in the Father's presence was his delight, his privilege, his lifeblood. This time of prayer filled Jesus up. It restored his soul and refreshed his spirit. It provided essential nurture and strength and guidance.

For Jesus, taking time to be with the Father, taking time to be still in the Father's presence, to pour out his heart to the Father, to bring his needs to the Father, to lift praise and thanksgiving to the Father, all of this was essential not optional. It was essential for a full and healthy life. Prayer was a priority for Jesus because the Father was a priority for Jesus.

And Jesus was the Son of God. How much more do I need to prioritize time alone with the Father—time in the secret place?

Chapter 19

NEVER GIVE UP!

And he told them a parable to the effect that they ought always to pray and not lose heart.
—Luke 18:1

One of the biggest challenges in prayer comes when we have prayed for something for a long time and yet there is still no breakthrough. At these times, it is difficult *not* to lose heart.

Perhaps it is prayer for an unsaved father. You've prayed, and you've prayed. You've prayed with all your heart. You've prayed, not just for years, but for decades. It is hard not to grow weary and give up. You wonder: "I have prayed day after day, week after week, month after month, year after year. Does all my praying make any difference at all? Does God care? Will God intervene? Does God even hear my prayers?" At times, all of us face this challenge. Most of us live with several of these long-standing prayers.

Jesus addressed this problem so strongly in Luke 18:1–8. He tells a parable about a wicked judge and a mistreated widow. The widow had been taken advantage of, and she goes to the judge to plead her case. Widows in that day had no clout, no legal rights, no privileges. They were completely vulnerable. Furthermore, this judge is arrogant and uncaring. He is despised, despicable, disgraceful. He doesn't care.

Yet the widow *wears him down.* Finally, he exclaims, *"Though I neither fear God nor respect man, yet because this widow keeps bothering me, I will give her justice, so that she will not beat me down by her continual coming"* (Luke 18:4–5).

By this point in the story, we are perplexed. We think to ourselves: "Is Jesus comparing God the Father to a wicked judge? Is Jesus comparing us to a mistreated widow who means nothing to the judge? Is Jesus saying that our praying is simply a matter of wearing God down?"

Jesus was a master storyteller. Let's be clear on what he is saying and what he is not saying in this story. First, consider the judge. This is not comparison, but contrast. If the harsh and uncaring judge came through, then how much more will our kind and loving Father, the Almighty God, come through for us? Repeatedly, Jesus teaches us that God is Father, a wise and loving Father, perfect in all his ways. This parable is contrast—jarring contrast.

But there is subtlety here: Jesus is exposing the lies we believe about God. How many of us view God as uncaring, inattentive, harsh—rather like this judge?

There was a chaplain at Harvard who was told by a student, "I don't believe in God." The chaplain wisely responded, "Tell me about this God you don't believe in. What's he like?" So many of us hold to a caricature of God rather than see God the way he is.

And then there's the widow. Is that who we are? Are we complete strangers, unknown and unimportant? No, it's just the opposite. We are God's much-loved children, his chosen and adopted children. In fact, in this very parable, Jesus will refer to us as his elect, his chosen ones. *"Will not God give justice to his elect, who cry to him day and night* (Luke18:7)?

It is certainly that way with me and my grandchildren. When one of them comes to me with a request, I want to say yes if at all possible. My grandchildren are not a nuisance but a delight. They are not strangers, unknown and unimportant. They are my much-loved grandchildren. This is exactly the way God sees us and the way he treats us. The point of this parable with the unimportant widow is not comparison, but contrast.

But perhaps the strongest thing about the story comes in verse 1, *before* the story. *"And he told them a parable to the effect that they ought always to pray and not lose heart"* (Luke 18:1). This hardly ever happens with the parables of Jesus. In just about all his parables, Jesus tells us the story and then leaves it to us to understand the point. But not here. Jesus does not want us to miss this. We must not miss this; Jesus is telling you and me: "Pray and keep on praying. Do not lose heart. Do not grow weary. Do not give up."

The parable closes with a poignant question: *"When the Son of Man comes, will he find faith on earth"* (Luke 18:8)? It is significant that Jesus does *not* say: "When the Son of Man comes, will he find prayer on earth?" After all, the parable had been a call to prayer. But why does Jesus close the parable with the words: *"will he find faith on earth?"*

The answer is simple. Our persevering prayer is proof of our faith. We may not have perfect faith, but do we have enough faith to keep on praying? What about you? Have you been praying for something for a long time? Will Jesus find faith in you? Will you resolve to keep on praying and not lose heart?

One of Winston Churchill's greatest traits in World War II was his perseverance. He refused to surrender to Germany, when other voices were clamoring for Britain to make peace while they could. When Britain was the only holdout against the Nazi war machine, Churchill refused to give up. Against all odds, he led his country to persevere until the United States joined the war effort. Winston Churchill epitomized perseverance.

There is a classic story about a speech Churchill made late in his life. He returned to the military school that he had attended as a boy in order to make a speech. Here was the hero of the nation, and the greatest orator of his generation, coming to his old school to deliver a speech.

When the time for the speech came, the hero of World War II made his way slowly to the podium to deliver the speech. He looked the boys square in the face and proclaimed: "Young gentlemen, never give up! Never give up! Never give up! Never! Never! Never!" [49]And with that, the great man sat down. That was the entire speech! Churchill's purpose was to imprint on the young boys one unforgettable message.

This is the same message that God intends to imprint on our prayer life. Never give up.

Chapter 20

HOUSE OF PRAYER

My house shall be a house of prayer.
—Luke 19:46

Luke 21 records a piercing episode in the life of Jesus. He is on the temple mount, the most holy place in the city, the most holy place on the earth. For in the temple is the Holy of Holies, the single place on earth where the presence of God is focused.

At the beginning of Passover week, Jesus looks around and sees all the buying and selling taking place on the temple mount. There is a cacophony of sounds—merchants hawking their wares, animals bleating, people everywhere scurrying about, clamoring and shouting.

Jesus is filled with deep emotion, a holy anger and zeal for the Father's glory. That's when it happens. Jesus begins to drive the merchants and money changers out of the temple area. He forcefully quotes the Old Testament book of Isaiah: *"It is written, 'My house shall be a house of prayer, but you have made it a den of robbers'"* (Luke 19:46).

Jesus declares with all boldness and authority: *"It is written!"* If God says it, then that settles it. Then Jesus continues: *"My house shall be a house of prayer!"* Jesus is reaching back to Isaiah 56:7 to proclaim that the essence of the temple is prayer—prayer in all its forms. This would include worship, praise, thanksgiving, confession of sin, intercession, supplication, and inquiring of the Lord.

Many other activities took place in the temple, but the main activity, the foundational purpose, was prayer. The essence of the temple was *not* to be a house of teaching. Or a house of Scripture study. Or a house for helping the needy. Or a house for educating the children. Or a house for priestly ministry. None of these. These are all good things, but the purpose of the temple was prayer: *"My house shall be a house of prayer!"*

Of course, we no longer have a temple in Jerusalem. We as individual believers *are* the temple. And we together as the local church *are* the temple. Can there be any doubt that the church today in the New Testament, like the temple of yesterday in the Old Testament, must be a house of prayer? Can there be any doubt that prayer in the church, like prayer in the temple, is primary, not secondary? *"My house shall be a house of prayer!"*

When it comes to our church seeking to become a house of prayer, our journey began twenty-five years ago. In the first five years of our church, we gave attention to prayer, but we did nothing special. One day God brought a couple to our church, Don and Madeline Soula. Our church was filled with young people at the time, and Don and Madeline were much older than the average age of our attenders. Moreover, they told me later that they did not like our church when they visited. However, God had made it clear to them that this was the church for them.

So Don and Madeline began to worship at WoodsEdge with cheerful hearts. They were people of prayer, and their hearts for prayer began to rub off on the rest of us. They began to infect us with the disease called prayer! At one point Don suggested that I read a book on prayer by some pastor in Brooklyn that I had never heard of. The book was called *Fresh Wind, Fresh Fire*. It was written by Jim Cymbala, the pastor of Brooklyn Tabernacle.

The book tells the story of what God had done through an inner-city church in Brooklyn that became a house of prayer because of their desperateness and their weakness. The story read like it was right out of the book of Acts. I was blown away by it. I did not know that there were still churches in the United States that prayed like this. Cymbala described the early years of the church and their desperate situation. Heroin and crack cocaine were rampant in their neighborhood. The church had few people and little money. The little band of people were struggling to survive as a church, and Cymbala was deeply discouraged. Finally, he came to a pivotal moment in his ministry. Cymbala would later write:

> I despaired at the thought that my life might slip by without seeing God show himself mightily on our behalf. Carol and I didn't want merely to mark time. I longed and cried out for God to change everything—me, the church, our passion for people, our praying.

> One day I told the Lord that I would rather die than merely tread water throughout my career in the ministry . . . always preaching about the power of the Word and the Spirit, but never seeing it. I abhorred the thought of just having more church services. I hungered for God to break through in our lives and ministry.[50]

Those words deeply moved me. He continued:

> From this day on, the prayer meeting will be the barometer of our church. What happens on Tuesday night will be the gauge by which we will judge success or failure because that will be the measure by which God blesses us.
>
> If we call upon the Lord, he has promised in his Word to answer, to bring the unsaved to himself, to pour out his Spirit among us. If we don't call upon the Lord, he has promised nothing—nothing at all. It's as simple as that. No matter what I preach or what we claim to believe in our heads, the future will depend upon our times of prayer.
>
> This is the engine that will drive the church.[51]

The message of *Fresh Wind, Fresh Fire* began to marinate in my soul. A few years later, four of us in leadership at our church went on an annual staff retreat. This was August 2002. During the retreat, it became clear to each of us that in the coming ministry season, our primary focus as a church must be prayer.

Later that day I went out for an easy run. During the run, I felt that God put several specific things on my heart about prayer: Start writing a daily email devotional on prayer. Change the weekly staff prayer from a business meeting to a prayer meeting. Relaunch the weekly prayer meeting on Wednesday nights. Moreover, the senior pastor, me, was to start attending the prayer meeting each week.

At the time, none of us had any idea what God would do through the simple decision to elevate prayer. A heart for prayer began to take deep root in our lives and in our church. The entire trajectory of our church began to change. It turned out that this emphasis on prayer would not be for one ministry season, but simply the way we would do church from this point on. Over time, God gave us a burning desire to reflect the prayer life found in the early church in Acts. We too wanted to become a house of prayer. We wanted to fulfill the words of Jesus in Luke 19:46 that our church, WoodsEdge, become a house of prayer.

Some years later, we realized how much our church had changed since that milestone moment in August 2002. Here's just one example: Three months after our decision on prayer, God gave me a heart for missions. It happened to me in Istanbul, Turkey, standing on the roof of a hotel overlooking Old Istanbul and the Bosphorus Strait dividing Europe and Asia. I was looking down at all the people milling around the streets during Ramadan, and I was gripped with a passion for lost people in Turkey and for missions around the world. It was immediately clear to me that God had given me a new heart for the nations. It would soon become clear to others in our church and for the first time, we began to pursue missions in earnest.

But this new heart for missions had begun three months earlier with the decision to prioritize prayer. Eventually, I realized that the level of prayer in a church is like the level of water in a lake. If the water level rises, all the boats rise. It is the same with the church and prayer: When the prayer level rises, all the ministries rise.

It has now been over twenty years since that fateful August in 2002. Our weekly staff meeting is still a time of prayer and worship. Our Wednesday night prayer service has become the most loved service at WoodsEdge. It is a time filled with the presence of God, a passion for Jesus, and a strong expectation of faith. Our people gather to seek God's face and seek God's hand. We expect God to show up. By God's grace, we have seen so many people healed over the years because we have raised the prayer level in our church.

Since that time, we have enhanced prayer in many other ways. We have a prayer pastor, dedicated to raising the prayer level in our church. We have a dedicated prayer room on our campus. We have prayer partners at all our weekend services. Every Sunday we pray for another church during our services. We have an email prayer chain with hundreds of people on it. Our staff goes off-site three times a year and spends an entire day seeking God in prayer. In all these ways and more, we continue to pursue Christ's vision that we become a house of prayer.

In the early church described in the book of Acts, there was an urgency for prayer. Prayer was their lifeblood. This is the calling of Christ for every church today. *"My house shall be a house of prayer!"*

Chapter 21

THE GREATER WORK

All these with one accord were devoting themselves to prayer.
—Acts 1:14

The book of Acts is the thrilling story of the early church exploding from a small group of Jewish believers in Jerusalem to become a large, international, multilingual, multiethnic body of believers who are empowered by the Holy Spirit. Behind this miraculous movement was one thing: The early church was devoted to prayer.

They were devoted to prayer because they were devoted to God. The foundation of everything that happens in the book of Acts is prayer. At every crucial turning point in the book, whenever the kingdom advances, behind every movement is a praying church.

Whenever God's people come together and devote themselves to prayer, things begin to happen. God things. The Spirit comes in power. Christ is exalted. Lost people get saved. Sick people get healed. Lives are transformed. Breakthroughs occur.

To say that the first group of 120 believers in Jerusalem devoted themselves to prayer is to say that prayer became their characteristic activity and their most urgent action. Prayer became their way of life. This was not a momentary thing, a flash-in-the-pan thing; the early believers gave unceasing attention to prayer. It was a sustained devotion to seek God for the rest of their lives. They understood the truth of what Oswald Chambers would give voice to centuries later: "Prayer does not fit us for the greater work, prayer is the greater work."[52]

All through the book of Acts, we see the priority of prayer. There are fifty-eight references to prayer in the twenty-eight chapters in the book. Since Acts is the only book in the New Testament that gives us a history of the early church, God is telling us that this is what he wants his church to be all about. God wants every church to be devoted to prayer, because prayer is where the power is. Prayer is where the intimacy is. Every church must become a house of prayer.

Leonard Ravenhill wrote:

> The church has many organizers, but few agonizers; many who pay, but few who pray; many resters, but few wrestlers, many who are enterprising, but few who are interceding. A worldly Christian will stop praying and a praying Christian will stop worldliness.
>
> Tithes may build a church, but tears will give it life. That is the difference between the modern

church and the early church. In the matter of effective praying, never have so many left so much to so few.[53]

As Ravenhill put it more succinctly, but just as powerfully, "The self-sufficient do not pray, the self-satisfied will not pray, the self-righteous cannot pray."[54]

God uses people who pray. God uses churches that pray. Scottish writer Andrew Bonar said: "God likes to see his people shut up to this, that there is no hope but in prayer. Herein lies the church's power against the world."[55]

The early church understood that:

- Prayer propels the kingdom forward around the world.
- Prayer is where the power is.
- Prayer accesses omnipotence.
- Prayer changes history.
- Prayer is the real work.
- Prayer is the greatest privilege of mortal man.

The great British pastor, Charles Spurgeon, put it so memorably: "Whenever God is ready to do a great work, he first sets his people to pray."[56]

What does it look like for you and me to be devoted to prayer? God gives us no formula or checklist, and it will not be the same for each of us. But perhaps it would be helpful to ask ourselves a few questions:

- Do you spend unhurried time alone with the Lord each day in prayer and Bible reading?
- Do you see this time alone with God as *the* priority of your day and as *the* privilege of your life?

- Do you *wrestle* in intercession for other people? Are there times when you *agonize* in prayer?
- In your heart of hearts, do you see prayer as a preliminary activity before the real work? Or do you see prayer as the real work? The greater work?
- Do you pray at times that God would pour out a spirit of prayer in your church?

What kind of people are devoted to prayer like the early Christians were? The kind of people who are hungry for God. The kind of people who are desperate for God. The kind of people who long to be intimates of God. The kind of people who see the unseen spiritual battle raging all around us. The kind of people who understand that prayer is the great privilege of human life. The kind of people who long to see God do a mighty work in our midst.

May we be such a people.

Chapter 22

GOD IS PRESENT

And when they heard it, they lifted their voices together to God.
—Acts 4:24

A man sat at a metro station in Washington, DC, and started to play the violin. It was a cold January morning. He played six Bach pieces for a total of forty-five minutes. During that time, since it was rush hour, it was calculated that thousands of people went through the station, most of them on their way to work.

Three minutes went by, and a middle-aged man noticed that there was a musician playing. He slowed his pace and stopped for a few seconds, before hurrying on to meet his schedule.

A minute later, the violinist received his first dollar tip. A woman threw the money in the case, and without stopping, continued to walk. A few minutes later, someone leaned against the wall to listen to him, but the man looked at his watch and started to walk again. Clearly, he was late for work.

The one who paid the most attention was a three-year-old boy. His mother tugged him along, hurried, but the kid stopped to look at the violinist. Finally, the mother pushed hard, and the child continued to walk, turning his head all the time. This action was repeated by several other children. All the parents, without exception, forced them to move on.

In the forty-five minutes the musician played, only six people stopped and stayed for a while. About twenty gave him money and then continued to walk at their normal pace. He collected $32. When he finished playing and silence took over, no one noticed it. No one applauded, nor was there any recognition.

No one knew this, but the violinist who played that day was Joshua Bell, one of the most famous musicians in the world. He played one of the most intricate pieces ever written, with a violin that was worth 3.5 million dollars. Two days before playing in the Washington subway, Joshua Bell sold out a theater in Boston, and the seats averaged $100 each.

> People had an incredible opportunity to listen to a world-renowned musician for free, but they were completely oblivious that Joshua Bell was present in the subway station.[57]

This is a striking story, but here is something even more striking. As believers in Jesus Christ, God is present with us all the time. We are often oblivious to his presence, but he is right there in the room with us. Always. We can connect with him and call out to him, at any time.

Throughout the book of Acts, there are references to prayer because the early church was a people devoted to prayer. And of all the references to prayer in the book of Acts, the single most powerful prayer comes in Acts 4.

These are the early days of the church. Exciting things are happening. God has poured out his Spirit upon his people. Thousands have come to faith in Christ. Miracles have occurred. The love and generosity in the nascent biblical community have been intoxicating.

But now the disciples encounter their first major problem. Peter and John, two of the main leaders in the fledgling church, have been arrested for preaching Jesus. They have been examined, threatened, and now released by the ruling Sanhedrin, the same judicial body behind the execution of Jesus just a few months before.

The situation is tense and volatile. If the early Christians refuse to acquiesce to the threats to stop preaching Jesus, then more executions are probable. After all, the rulers of the nation did not hesitate to crucify Jesus. Would his followers be next?

In this dire situation, Peter and John report back to the church, explaining all that happened. And how does the church respond? *"And when they heard it, they lifted their voices together to God"* (Acts 4:24).

This is what people of faith do in desperate and dangerous circumstances. They call out to God. They call out to God immediately. They call out to God fervently. They call out to God together. They recognize that God is present—and they call out to him.

Can you imagine being present with the early church in Jerusalem that day as Peter and John describe their arrest and the threats made by the Sanhedrin? The place where the church gathered must have been electric—filled with God's presence.

How do most churches in the West respond today when they encounter overwhelming challenges or crises? Far too many churches respond by discussing, debating, analyzing, strategizing, organizing, and planning. Each of these activities has its place, but the early church's response to crisis was prayer. Prayer is their first response, their default response, their instinctive response.

They were too desperate *not* to pray.

Today, the church in the West has a formidable challenge. We have so many resources—money, education, buildings, contacts, and more—that we do not realize how much we need God. Furthermore, we lack the intense persecution that much of the world experiences. Therefore, our tendency in times of crisis is to pray a brief, preliminary prayer but then largely depend upon our own plans and resources. We sometimes forget that God is present in the room with us.

Oswald Chambers wrote:

> We tend to use prayer as a last resort, but God wants it to be our first line of defense. We pray when there's nothing else we can do, but God wants us to pray before we do anything at all.[58]

God uses people who pray. God uses churches that pray. God uses churches that pray as their first and instinctive response. In the early church, prayer was their first response, their immediate response, their instinctive response because they recognized that God is present.

Chapter 23

PRAYER AND THE WORD

*Who through the mouth of our father David, your servant,
said by the Holy Spirit.*
—Acts 4:25

Prayer and Scripture go together. This is one of the essential principles for prayer. We see the practice modeled throughout the Bible, including in this prayer by the gathered early church in Acts 4. The early church is praying together when someone quotes Scripture. The quoted passage is found in Psalm 2, and it was quite likely cited from memory.

Here's the prayer:

> *Sovereign Lord, who made the heaven and the earth and the sea and everything in them, who through the mouth of our father David, your servant, said by the Holy Spirit, "Why did the Gentiles rage, and the peoples plot in vain? The kings of the earth set themselves, and the rulers were gathered together, against the Lord and against his Anointed."*
> —Acts 4:24–26

They were quoting God's Word to God. God never tires of hearing his Word prayed back to him, because it shows that we take his Word seriously, and we are claiming his Word for our own lives. God loves it when we infuse our prayers with Scripture. The Spirit of God uses the Word of God to shape our prayers to God.

Our Bible reading shapes and infuses our prayer. Conversely, our prayer completes and enriches our Bible reading. They go together. The Word of God is vital to prayer, just as prayer is vital to the Word of God. The Word shows us how to pray; prayer helps us understand the Word. The Word shows us who God is; prayer accesses God's power. Reading the Word shapes our praying; our praying enriches our reading the Word.

Prayer and the Word of God go together. What God has joined together let no man separate.

When you read the Bible, pray as you read it. Pray for wisdom, for insight, for understanding, for application.

Agree with the Scripture. Dialogue with God. Make it a conversation:

> "Yes, Lord, make it so."
> "Oh yes, Lord. You can do it."
> "Forgive me, Lord."

You are not merely reading a book of theology and truths about God. You are reading God's Word, which is alive and active and empowered by the Holy Spirit. You are reading love letters from your Father. You are meeting with God. You ask God to speak to you through his Word, and then you, in turn, pour out your heart to God. Pray your way through Scripture.

Eugene Peterson, the translator of *The Message,* noted:

> The Scriptures, read and prayed, are our primary and normative access to God as he reveals himself to us. The Scriptures are our listening post for learning the language of the soul, the ways God speaks to us; they also provide the vocabulary and grammar that are appropriate for us as we in our turn speak to God. Prayer detached from Scripture, from listening to God, disconnected from God's words to us, short-circuits the relational language that is prayer. Christians acquire this personal and relational practice of prayer primarily (although not exclusively) under the shaping influence of the Psalms and Jesus.[59]

Andrew Murray, a South African pastor and writer, made the same point:

> Prayer and the Word of God are inseparable, and should always go together in the quiet time of the inner chamber. This really gives prayer its power, that I take God's thoughts from his Word and present them before him. How indispensable God's Word is for all true prayer.[60]

Then there's the example of George Müller who lived an incredible life. He pastored the same church in Bristol, England, for sixty years during the 1800s. He founded an orphanage and provided for thousands of orphans and never asked anyone for money. Yet his orphans never missed a meal. He founded the orphanage, not so much to take care of the orphans, but to provide an example to Christians that God is a prayer-hearing God. Most importantly, Müller *knew* God—intimately.

This was Müller's approach in his time with God, as seen in his autobiography. Note the emphasis on Scripture though he was known as a man of prayer.

> The primary business I must attend to every day is to fellowship with the Lord. The first concern is not how much I might serve the Lord, but how my inner man might be nourished. I may share the truth with the unconverted; I may try to encourage believers; I may relieve the distressed; or I may, in other ways, seek to behave as a child of God;

yet, not being happy in the Lord and not being nourished and strengthened in my inner man day by day, may result in this work being done in the wrong spirit.

The most important thing I had to do was to read the Word of God and to meditate on it. Thus my heart might be comforted, encouraged, warned, reproved, and instructed.

Formerly, when I rose, I began to pray as soon as possible. But I often spent a quarter of an hour to an hour on my knees struggling to pray while my mind wandered. Now I rarely have this problem. As my heart is nourished by the truth of the Word, I am brought into true fellowship with God. I speak to my Father and to my Friend (although I am unworthy) about the things that He has brought before me in His precious Word.

It often astonishes me that I did not see the importance of meditation upon Scripture earlier in my Christian life. As the outward man is not fit for work for any length of time unless he eats, so it is with the inner man. What is the food for the inner man? Not prayer, but the Word of God—not the simple reading of the Word of God, so that it only passes through our minds, just as water runs through a pipe. No, we must consider what we read, ponder over it, and apply it to our hearts.[61]

You may not choose to follow Muller's precise approach, beginning with Scripture reading. That is not my current practice. But our Scripture reading should lead to prayer, and our prayer should be infused with Scripture. Pray as you read, and read as you pray.

Chapter 24

BOLD PRAYER

*And now, Lord, look upon their threats and grant to your
servants to continue to speak your word with all boldness,
while you stretch out your hand to heal,
and signs and wonders are performed through the
name of your holy servant Jesus.*
—Acts 4:29–30

This is one more principle from the remarkable prayer in Acts 4. This principle shows us what the early church prayed for in crisis and what they did *not* pray for.

The young church has just heard the startling news: Peter and John have been threatened by the supreme court of Israel, demanding they must stop preaching Jesus. Life and death are at stake for Peter, for John, for every believer in Jerusalem.

The church gathers, and immediately they call out to God. They begin with the greatness of God, praising God as the sovereign Lord. Then they continue praying by quoting Scripture, a passage from Psalm 2 that continues to underscore that God alone is sovereign. Finally, they come to their petition. What will they ask the Lord for?

Most of us would be asking for protection. For safety. For deliverance from the Sanhedrin and from the Romans. Certainly, if I had been there, I would have been praying like this: "Lord, deliver us! Lord, protect us! Lord, stop those enemies and change their hearts!"

And if we had been praying that way, there would be nothing wrong with it. Throughout Scripture, there are examples of praying for protection and deliverance. In fact, King David prays that way throughout the Psalms. We must be clear: There is nothing wrong with praying for safety—nothing at all. We should pray for safety. Indeed, many times this is the proper expression of trust in our God. But that is not the Spirit-led prayer of the early church on this occasion.

They do not say a word about their safety, at least none recorded in Scripture. They were so intent on the gospel. They were so focused on the kingdom. They were so preoccupied with reaching lost people. These Jesus-intoxicated, Spirit-empowered believers were so kingdom-preoccupied that it was natural for them to pray: "Lord, advance your kingdom! Lord, give us boldness! Lord, save lost people!" These were men and women who had seen the risen Jesus. These were men and women who had been filled to the brim with the Spirit of God, and they could not get over it.

But they are not done asking. Look again at their prayer:

And now, Lord, look upon their threats and grant to your servants to continue to speak your word with all boldness, while you stretch out your hand to heal, and signs and wonders are performed through the name of your holy servant Jesus.
—Acts 4:29–30

That is a big prayer . . . a bold prayer! "Lord, heal. Lord, do the miraculous. Lord, do the impossible." When you pray to a big God, make your prayers big. Make your prayers bold. Make your prayers God-sized. Ask for the sorts of things that only God can do, the sorts of things that if God does not answer, then you don't have a chance on your own.

Whenever I am praying with others, and someone makes a big, bold request, I smile inside. I love it—and I can only imagine that God loves it too.

We must ever remember God's message to us in Ephesians 3:20–21:

Now to him who is able to do far more abundantly than all that we ask or think, according to the power at work within us, to him be glory in the church and in Christ Jesus throughout all generations, forever and ever. Amen.

Over the years I have often reminded our congregation of what A. W. Tozer said:

Anything God has ever done, he can do now. Anything God has ever done anywhere, he can do here. Anything that God has ever done for anyone, he can do for you.[62]

What God did with the early Christians in Jerusalem in the first century, God can do with us in our day. Maybe here is the question for us: What are we trusting God for that only God can do?

How does God respond to early church's bold request? This is the best part! God seems to express his deep pleasure in a most striking way: *"And when they had prayed, the place in which they were gathered together was shaken, and they were all filled with the Holy Spirit and continued to speak the word of God with boldness"* (Acts 4:31).

The place is shaken. God is letting them know: "I hear your prayers. I will answer your prayers. I will rescue you. And I will give you what you ask for. For I am a prayer-hearing God." The kingdom of God continued to advance in Jerusalem despite the persecution and threats. It continued to advance because the early church continued to speak God's Word with boldness. They continued to speak God's Word with boldness because they were all filled with the Holy Spirit. They were all filled with the Holy Spirit because they were a people devoted to prayer.

In the book of Acts, at every critical juncture where the kingdom of God advances, the church is praying. Foundational to kingdom advance is a people devoted to prayer. All through the book of Acts, God is teaching us—you and me—the priority of prayer, the power of prayer, the urgency of prayer. He is teaching us that he is a prayer-hearing God.

It is as if God is saying to you and to me through Scripture: "Call out to me. Whatever the need is, whatever the problem is, whatever the fear is, call out to me. Call out to me first. Call out to me together. Call out to me with all your hearts. Call out to me."

CHAPTER 25

THE 6:4 CALLING

*But we will devote ourselves to prayer and to the
ministry of the word.*
—Acts 6:4

In Acts 6 we see the inspiring early church, with God's anointing upon them and exploding with growth. Yet they too had challenges, including the problems of division and grumbling because the serving of meals to widows was not equitable. So the twelve apostles, the leaders in the church, take decisive action.

Note carefully what the apostles do *not* do. They do not jump right in and start serving the meals themselves. That was not their calling. Their calling was to pray and teach the Word.

It was not that their calling of prayer and the Word was better than the calling of serving tables. It was not better; it was just different. Every calling from God is sacred, whether it is praying or washing dishes. The apostles were crystal clear on their calling: "This is what God has called us to do—pray and teach the Word. God has called other people to make sure that the meals are distributed fairly. So choose seven men among yourselves who can lead this ministry. But as for us, we will continue our calling to focus on prayer and Scripture."

Part of the satanic attack against the early church in Jerusalem was to distract the apostles from their calling. If Satan could sidetrack the apostles to neglect prayer and the Bible, then the entire church would become spiritually malnourished. This remains a satanic scheme against the church in our day.

The early church faced the problem of division and complaining head-on. The apostles address this challenge; they stick to their own calling from God, and they equip other godly men for the ministry with the widows. The result is found in verse 7 of Acts 6: *"And the word of God continued to increase, and the number of the disciples multiplied greatly in Jerusalem, and a great many of the priests became obedient to the faith."* Verse 7 emphasizes, three times, the growth of the church:

- The Word of God continued to increase.
- The number of disciples multiplied greatly in Jerusalem.
- A great many of the priests became obedient to the faith.

Can you imagine how exciting, how electric, must have been the atmosphere in the early church in Jerusalem? This is nothing less than the outbreak of revival. God is teaching us that the most fertile soil for revival is when the leaders of the church focus on prayer and the Word, while they empower other gifted people to do the various ministries in the church. (See also Ephesians 4:11–12.)

The early church grew from 120 believers at the beginning of Acts 1 to 3,000 believers by the end of Acts 2; then 5,000 more men plus women and children were added in Acts 3. New believers were added to the church daily. By the time this passage in Acts 6 was written, there were probably 15,000 to 20,000 people in the church.

The size of the church is not the issue. The only issue is this: "Are there any lost people out there who need to be reached? Are there any lost people on our street, in our apartment complex, in our workplace, in our fitness class, wherever we live?" The leaders in the Jerusalem church heeded their calling to focus on prayer and the Word. God honored it in a dramatic way.

It is an occupational hazard for us pastors to neglect our personal relationship with the Lord. We are constantly doing work *for* God, and we think that translates automatically into greater love for God. But that is not true. God has called pastors primarily to be *lovers* of God not *workers* for God. We can get so busy doing the work of ministry that we neglect our own relationship with God.

The apostles in the early church did not make this mistake. They recognized that their calling was not to solve all the problems and do all the work but to empower the entire body to do the work of ministry. Meanwhile, they would focus on their calling—prayer and the Word of God.

We have more than enough pastors who are marvelously gifted, yet they have a shallow spiritual life because they fail to prioritize, above all other things, their own personal time with the Lord.

If pastors neglect God, then their ministries will lack depth and authenticity. There will be the unmistakable aroma of phoniness, and those pastors will eventually burn out or crash.

The first duty for the pastor is to love Jesus and seek his face. Not his hand. His face. (This is true for every believer, but especially so for spiritual leaders.) Jesus did this. Paul did this. The early church did this. Why would we think we don't need this time alone with the Lord?

Oswald Chambers hit the bull's-eye: "It is impossible for a believer, no matter what his experience, to keep right with God if he will not take the trouble to spend time with God. Spend plenty of time with God; let other things go, but don't neglect him."[63]

This must begin with pastors. As go the pastors, so goes the church. If we hope to see a revival in our country today, it will not be because we discover a fancy new technique or method. It will not be because we have fancier buildings and more money. It will be because pastors across American rediscover the 6:4 priority. This led to revival in the first church. It can lead to revival in our church today.

Chapter 26

FERVENT UNITED PRAYER

So Peter was kept in prison, but earnest prayer for him was made to God by the church.
—Acts 12:5

The book of Acts is replete with wonderful references to prayer. However, there is only one chapter in Acts where prayer is the focus throughout the chapter. That chapter is Acts 12, which records a time of grave crisis in the church.

First, the Apostle James is executed by King Herod. Then Peter is arrested, and it seems like Peter will be next to be executed. Then we read: *"But earnest prayer for him was made to God by the church"* (Acts 12:5).

Earnest prayer! Fervent prayer! This is the kind of prayer that we see from Elijah in James 5:17: *"Elijah was a man with a nature like ours, and he prayed fervently that it might not rain, and for three years and six months it did not rain on the earth."*

This is the kind of prayer that is from Jesus in Hebrews 5:7: *"In the days of his flesh, Jesus offered up prayers and supplications, with loud cries and tears, to him who was able to save him from death, and he was heard because of his reverence."*

Fervent prayer is when you pray wholeheartedly. You are not halfhearted about it. Your prayer is not mechanical or mindless. What is it about earnest prayer that pleases God? Why does God want us to pray earnestly, fervently?

First, God does not want anything from us that is just mindless or empty ritual. In Matthew 15, Jesus quotes the prophet Isaiah about mindless prayer or worship:

> *You hypocrites! Well did Isaiah prophesy of you, when he said:*
>
> *"'This people honors me with their lips, but their heart is far from me; in vain do they worship me, teaching as doctrines the commandments of men.'"*
>
> —Matthew 15:7–9

They had the words, but their heart was not in it.

If we come to God in prayer and recognize just who it is that we are talking to—the sovereign, holy, almighty God who loves us outrageously—then it will be difficult to pray without our heart in it.

John Bunyan, author of *The Pilgrim's Progress,* wrote: "When you pray, rather let your heart be without words than your words without heart."[64]

Charles Spurgeon described earnest prayer in this way: "Prayer pulls the rope down below and the great bell rings above in the ears of God. Some scarcely stir the bell, for they pray so languidly; others give only an occasional jerk at the rope. But he who communicates with heaven is the one who grasps the rope boldly and pulls continuously with all his might."[65]

Let me ask you: How do you pull the rope of prayer? Do you barely move the rope, or do you pull it with all your might? Do you pray earnestly? I am not suggesting that we pray theatrically, for show or performance. That's the opposite of the point. But with God as our only audience, do we pray from our heart, and with all our heart?

Of course, when it comes to prayer, the early church had one distinct advantage over the American church today. One of their leaders had just been executed. Whenever one of the leaders in the church gets their head cut off, everybody else becomes more interested in prayer. Persecution fuels the flame of prayer. If a serious persecution breaks out against the church in the United States, it will be extremely difficult, but it will also add fuel to the flame of prayer. In his superb book, *Prayer*, Tim Keller relates this story:

> Ethelfrith, the pagan Saxon king of Northumbria, had invaded Wales and was about to give battle. The Welsh were Christians, and as Ethelfrith was observing the army of his opponents spread out before him, he noticed a host of unarmed men. When he asked who they were, he was told that they were the Christian monks of Bangor, praying for the success of their army. Ethelfrith immediately realized the seriousness of the situation. "Attack them first," he ordered.[66]

The non-Christians of the world often have more respect for the "sturdy reality" of prayer than we do. The power of prayer "is no fiction, whatever we may think of it."[67]

A second characteristic of prayer found in Acts 12 is that the believers prayed together. God loves it whenever his people pray, but he seems especially delighted when his people pray together. So many of the prayers in the Bible are public prayers, corporate prayers, prayers together. This is true for most prayers in the book of Psalms. It is true of the Lord's Prayer when Jesus taught us how to pray. He did not say "My Father," but "*Our* Father." He taught us to say, "Give *us*," "Forgive *us*," "Lead *us* not." He assumed prayer together.

At the outset of the book of Acts, we read of their prayer together. *"All these with one accord were devoting themselves to prayer, together with the women and Mary the mother of Jesus, and his brothers"* (Acts 1:14). At other times, we see the early church praying together, including at this time of crisis in Acts 12.

To be clear, God loves individual prayer. Personal prayer is essential to our spiritual lives. But there seems to be a special anointing when God's people pray together.

What happens after the believers begin praying? God responds—dramatically. Peter is miraculously rescued by an angel. Puritan theologian Thomas Watson remarked, "The angel fetched Peter from the prison, but it was prayer fetched the angel."[68] Think of the massive power behind Herod—the power of the state, the power of the army, the power of the Emperor. But who had the real power in this situation? The intercessors. Prayer is where the power is because prayer touches omnipotence.

Then Peter shows up at the house where the church is praying. The response is hilarious. First, Rhoda hears Peter's voice and is so excited she forgets to open the door for him, but instead runs to tell the church. But the church does not believe her. *"They said to her, 'You are out of your mind.' But she kept insisting that it was so, and they kept saying, 'It is his angel'"* (Acts 12:15)!

Can you picture this? They are praying desperately: "Lord, please rescue Peter! Lord, you can do it! Lord, you can do all things! Just release Peter from that prison!" Then when God answers prayer and Peter shows up, how do they respond? "Oh, Rhoda, don't be silly. It cannot be Peter. No way is it Peter!" Unfortunately, we do the same thing at times, and don't really expect God to come through. I imagine they later had a good laugh at themselves.

Doesn't this passage encourage you? God answers their prayer even though they were riddled with doubt. But they had enough faith to pray. And God says yes despite their doubt. Friend, maybe you are like the Christians in Acts 12 at times. Maybe you have a little bit of faith and a whole lot of doubt. But if you have enough faith to call out to God, then God will hear you, and he might well do a miracle.

What is the biggest miracle in your life that you need right now? Pause now and ask God to do that miracle.

Consider this quote on prayer from writer and busy mom Ann Voskamp:

> The only thing that prevents me from praying more is me. It's my own inflated sense of self-importance, the elevation of my work, of my agenda, that keeps me from prayer-communion.

That's called idol worship. I don't pray enough because I'm practicing idol worship. I can hardly look him in the eye. It's a startling, wrenching thing to discover that it's not time, or busyness, or pressing concerns that prevent one from prayer.

The extent of prayer in one's life is a direct function of whether something else has been set up as more important than God.[69]

These words are so convicting. O Lord, change us. I love the early church in Jerusalem. They were devoted to prayer because they were devoted to God.

Chapter 27

THIS IS HOW WE FIGHT OUR BATTLES

Praying at all times in the Spirit, with all prayer and supplication. To that end, keep alert with all perseverance, making supplication for all the saints.
—Ephesians 6:18

The classic passage on the spiritual battle is found in Ephesians 6. In this passage, Paul lists six pieces of armor: the belt of truth, the breastplate of righteousness, shoes of the gospel, shield of faith, helmet of salvation, sword of the Spirit.

Then he comes to prayer. However, prayer is not the seventh piece of armor, but what undergirds all the armor. Prayer is how we fight the battle. Prayer is how we live the Christian life. Prayer pervades all we do.

The call to prayer in Ephesians 6 is such a strong, stirring call: *"Praying at all times in the Spirit, with all prayer and supplication. To that end, keep alert with all perseverance, making supplication for all the saints."* Because we are in a cosmic spiritual battle, because demons are scheming to ruin us, because the devil is a prowling lion looking for someone to devour, prayer must be a priority—*an urgent priority*.

If God pulled back the curtain to reveal the spiritual realm, including all the angels of God and all the demons of hell, no one would have to tell us to pray. Heaven will be a party, but life here is a battle, a spiritual battle. This is why the call to prayer is so strong in Ephesians 6. Four times Paul uses the emphatic term *all*. Let's unpack each one of these.

1. *Praying at all times in the Spirit." All* times. Clearly, this does not mean 24-7 nonstop prayer. We must sleep and do other things. But our life is lived in the presence of God. He is always with us, in us. We have a continual, ongoing conversation with the Lord.

    Often, we bring requests to him, sing to him, or call out to him. But much of the time, we are alert to listen to him, alert to his leadings and promptings. Or we are simply living life in his presence, soaking in his love.

    The essence of prayer is not asking for things, but it is being with Father, drawing close, connecting, letting him love you. The heart of real prayer is not religious activity, but a love affair with the God of the universe.

    Because of the cosmic spiritual war, it is vital that we pray *in the Spirit*. Our prayer must flow out of a

Spirit-led, Spirit-filled, Spirit-empowered life. The Spirit *prompts* our prayer, *fuels* our prayer, *guides* our prayer. We pray in the Spirit.

2. *"With all prayer and supplication."* This includes worship, praise, singing, thanksgiving. At times it includes confession, silence, and listening. At times this includes loud cries and petitions, either for yourself or for others.

3. *"To that end, keep alert with all perseverance."* Keep alert. There is urgency in the air; bullets are flying, bombs exploding, soldiers bleeding. Lives are at stake; souls are at stake.

   In the fifteenth century, Thomas à Kempis wrote: "The devil sleepeth not, neither is the flesh as yet dead, therefore cease not to prepare thyself for the battle, for on thy right hand and on thy left are enemies who never rest."[70] Never underestimate the power of prayer. For prayer is the main work we do. Lord Tennyson famously noted: "More things are wrought by prayer than this world dreams of."[71]

   Maybe you've prayed for the salvation of a friend or loved one for years—or even for decades. Never give up. Remember the challenge of Luke 18:1: *"And he told them a parable to the effect that they ought always to pray and not lose heart."* There is something about persevering prayer that pleases our heavenly Father.

4. *"Making supplication for all the saints."* This is the ministry of intercession. There is no more important ministry—for family, for friends, for church, for missionaries, for strangers.

But intercession is hard work. The founder of Dallas Theological Seminary, Lewis Sperry Chafer, wrote, "Prayer is hard work, and we are inherently lazy."[72]

William Booth, the founder of the Salvation Army noted:

> You must pray with all your might. That does not mean saying your prayers, or sitting gazing about in church or chapel with eyes wide open while someone else says them for you.
>
> It means fervent, effectual, untiring wrestling with God. This kind of prayer be sure the devil and the world and your own indolent, unbelieving nature will oppose. They will pour water on this flame.[73]

Walter Wink observed, "History belongs to the intercessors, who believe the future into being."[74]

Church, this is how we fight our battles.

Chapter 28

LIFEBLOOD

And so, from the day we heard, we have not ceased to pray for you.
—Colossians 1:9

I am astounded by what Paul says to the Colossian Christians in this verse. He is saying to them, "From the day I first heard about you coming to Christ, I began praying for you. And I have prayed for you ever since without ceasing."

When Paul first heard the news about them coming to Christ, he began praying for them. He prayed for their spiritual life, for their walk with Jesus, that they would know God better, and that they would be filled with God's joy. Since he says he has not ceased praying for them, this probably means that he has prayed for them at least every day and perhaps several times a day. He prays for them all the time.

If Paul had planted the church in Colossae, it would still be impressive that he prayed for them without ceasing. Or, if Paul had pastored the church in Colossae for a season, it would be highly significant that he has continued to pray for them without ceasing. However, Paul did not plant this church. Paul never pastored this church. Paul had never even visited this church. He has never met these people. Yet Paul can write: "I have not stopped praying for you since I first heard about you coming to faith."

Why does Paul pray for the Colossian Christians this way? Why does he pray without ceasing for a people that he has never even met? Because Paul knew the power of prayer. Paul knew that prayer is where the life change is, that prayer is where the breakthrough is. Paul knew that prayer is the main work, the greater work. Paul knew that the best thing—the most loving thing—that he could do for any people was to pray for them.

Keep in mind that Paul was a brilliant theologian. Remember that he wrote much of the New Testament, that he preached the gospel all over the Empire, that he had planted churches all over. In fact, Paul was used by God more significantly than anyone since Christ. However, Paul knew that prayer was the real work. The essence of Paul's ministry was not his preaching or his leading or his discipling or his church planting. The essence of his ministry was his praying. Paul's method of ministry was prayer.

If the modern church wants to do church the way Paul did church, if the modern church wants to do ministry the way the early church did ministry, then we will focus on prayer. Prayer is the lifeblood of a church.

This may not be the way the modern American church does church. But this is the way that Paul did church. This is the way that the early church did church. This is the New Testament way of doing church.

CHAPTER 29

THE PRAYER OF EPAPHRAS

Epaphras, who is one of you, a servant of Christ Jesus, greets you, always struggling on your behalf in his prayers.
—Colossians 4:12

You've got to love Epaphras. He is from the city of Colossae, but when Colossians is written, he is with Paul in Rome. Yet his heart is still in Colossae, with his people. So he prays for them. And how he prays.

Colossians 4:12 tells us that Epaphras is not simply going through the motions of prayer. This is not mechanical prayer or lifeless prayer. No, he is struggling for them in prayer. He is agonizing for them in prayer. He is working hard for them in prayer. He's pouring his heart out to God on their behalf. He's going to battle. He's storming the gates.

He's praying with heart, life, and passion: "O God, please intervene for these people. Lord, you've got to protect them from the false teachers. Lord, you've got to be with them. And bless them. And protect them. Lord, may they love you more. Lord, bless the church in Colossae."

Epaphras was struggling for them in prayer. He was agonizing for them in prayer. He could not pray dry, boring prayers because lives were at stake. Marriages were at stake. Children were at stake. Eternities were at stake. The stakes were just too high for lifeless, lukewarm prayer.

But the text does not merely say that Epaphras was struggling in prayer for them. The text says that Epaphras was *always* struggling in prayer for them. He doesn't just pray for them on occasion—once in a while. He prays for them always. Day in, day out, without ceasing. Just like Paul did.

Why? Why does Epaphras pray this way? Because he knew that prayer changes lives. Epaphras knew God was a prayer-hearing God. He knew that if you want to see a breakthrough, it happens through prayer. Epaphras knew that prayer is the slender nerve that unleashes the omnipotent power of God.

Paul also was an intercessor. For example, in Colossians 1:9, he writes: *"And so, from the day we heard, we have not ceased to pray for you."* Like Epaphras, Paul prays for the believers in Colossae. Not only does Paul pray for them, but he prays for them constantly, without ceasing. And not only does he pray for them constantly, but he *tells* them that he prays for them constantly.

Paul must have known that these believers, whom he had never met, would be encouraged from the depths of their hearts, to know that the Apostle Paul regularly prayed for them.

In the fall of 1972, I met John Lodwick, a fellow freshman at Rice University. Little did I know that John and I would become fast friends and room together for the next eight years, throughout college and graduate school.

Sometime after meeting John, I began praying for him every day. Perhaps it was in the first weeks or in the first months after meeting him; I no longer remember. But I began praying for him every day. I have done that now for over fifty years, and I will continue to pray for John for the rest of my years on earth. John is a close friend, and prayer is the single most important thing I can do for him.

Moreover, not only do I pray for John daily, but John prays for me. I know he does. And from time to time, he tells me that he prays for me daily. I already know it but still it is good to hear it afresh, "I'm praying for you daily."

Just as Paul prayed continually for the Christians at Colossae and just as Epaphras prayed continually for the Christians at Colossae, and just as John Lodwick prays continually for me, let's pray continually for the people God puts on our hearts. And let's tell them we are praying for them. They will be encouraged from the depths of their hearts.

Back to the example of Epaphras always struggling in prayer for the Colossians: What would it be like to have an Epaphras praying for you? It would be pretty sweet, wouldn't it? What would it be like if we had a whole church full of

Epaphrases praying for us, and for our church, and for our city, and for our country? We would see breakthroughs like we've never seen before.

We would see many more people coming to Christ, marriages restored, miraculous healings, breakthroughs for our kids. We would see more of everything we want to see—if we had a whole church full of Epaphrases calling out to God.

Are you willing to be one of those Epaphrases because prayer is so powerful?

Chapter 30

A WAY OF LIFE

Pray without ceasing.
—1 Thessalonians 5:17

This three-word command seems impossible at first glance, yet we know that our Father doesn't give us commands to defeat and frustrate us. He gives us commands for our good.

What is God telling us here? He is telling us to be in an attitude of prayer all the time. Live your life in the presence of God. Realize that God is right there with you throughout the day and night. Sense, remember, and enjoy his presence. Talk with him throughout the day. Make this a way of life.

To fully understand this crisp command, let's remember what Paul said to other churches. In Romans 1:9–10, he expressed his heart to the Christians in Rome:

> *For God is my witness, whom I serve with my spirit in the gospel of his Son, that without ceasing I mention you always in my prayers, asking that somehow by God's will I may now at last succeed in coming to you.*

Similarly, in Colossians 1:9, he wrote:

> *And so, from the day we heard, we have not ceased to pray for you, asking that you may be filled with the knowledge of his will in all spiritual wisdom and understanding.*

Then again in 1 Thessalonians 1:2–3, Paul stated:

> *We give thanks to God always for all of you, constantly mentioning you in our prayers, remembering before our God and Father your work of faith and labor of love and steadfastness of hope in our Lord Jesus Christ.*

Finally, in 2 Timothy 1:3 he wrote this to his spiritual son Timothy:

> *I thank God whom I serve, as did my ancestors, with a clear conscience, as I remember you constantly in my prayers night and day.*

So, in four places in the New Testament, Paul states that he is praying for a church *without ceasing*. Certainly, Paul does not mean that he prays for these 24-7 nonstop. Clearly, he sleeps. He writes. He speaks. When he is praying unceasingly for one church, he cannot be praying unceasingly for another.

Does Paul not mean that he prays for the Romans all the time? That he prays for the Colossian Christians frequently? That he prays for the Thessalonian Christians regularly? That he often prays for Timothy? I think that through these commands, God is telling us to be in an attitude of prayer all the time, to sense his presence, to remember his presence, to enjoy his presence. He wants us to talk with him a lot throughout the day.

In other words, we should have an ongoing conversation with God—talking, listening, singing, thanking, asking, interceding, praising, confessing, laughing, weeping. Ours is to be a life lived in God's presence, enjoying God throughout the day.

Maybe it's a bit like a persistent cough. That cough is in your throat throughout the day, ready to erupt in an actual cough at any moment. Similarly, we are in an attitude of prayer throughout the day, ready to erupt in an actual prayer at any moment.

We're driving to work, talking with God about our day, about a project, about a conflict, about an important meeting. As we're playing with our preschooler on the living room floor, we breathe a prayer of thanksgiving. When we're at our desk working away, we pray for wisdom at various points. As we're walking to our car and remember a friend who needs a job, we lift our friend's need up to God. While we're driving to the grocery store listening to worship music on our smartphone, we sing to God.

It's life lived before God. It's not a burden. It's not so much a discipline to practice, but an attitude to adopt. "God is here, with me, right now, and all the time!"

The British writer G. K. Chesterton caught the spirit of this command when he wrote about thanksgiving:

> You say grace before meals. All right. But I say grace before the concert and the opera, and grace before the play and pantomime, and grace before I open a book, and grace before sketching, painting, swimming, fencing, boxing, walking, playing, dancing and grace before I dip the pen in the ink.[75]

Paul prayed without ceasing. There are not too many things we do without ceasing throughout the day. But there is one thing that so many of us do, so many Americans do. We check our phones. So many of us walk around with our phones in our hand, frequently looking down at our phone. We're checking texts or email or voicemail or Instagram or Facebook or X (formerly Twitter) or TikTok. So many of us are always looking down at our phones rather than looking up to the Lord.

Could this be a scheme of the enemy to distract us from prayer? The cell phone is a good tool. But it is a bad master. If all of us raised the prayer level in our lives, praying fervently and frequently, would we not see more breakthroughs in our lives with our kids, our city, and our country?

The ideal for us is to make prayer without ceasing becomes a natural way of life. It might be helpful to have some routines or rhythms to help us. Here are some examples of practices to consider:

- Every time you get in your car, pray as soon as you close your car door.
- While you drive to work every morning, make that a time of intercession for family members and close friends.
- Make your daily exercise regimen a time of intercession for family, for your church, for close friends.
- While you make coffee every morning or do some other morning routine, sing to him.
- Every time you drive to a grocery store or do other routine shopping trips, give thanks to God all the way there and all the way back.

Perhaps these practices might help you cultivate a mindset to pray without ceasing.

Chapter 31

THANKSGIVING

Give thanks in all circumstances.
—1 Thessalonians 5:18

The Bible repeatedly and emphatically calls us to give thanks to God. For example, 1 Thessalonians 5:18 tells us: *"Give thanks in all circumstances; for this is the will of God in Christ Jesus for you."*

Why is this so important to God? Why does *my* gratitude matter to the sovereign and infinite God who created the galaxies?

- God deserves our gratitude. It's only right that we thank him. Everything good in our lives is a gift from God. Paul asks, *"What do you have that you did not receive"* (1 Corinthians 4:7)? The answer? Nothing. Nothing at all. God has been so good to us.

- We thank God because we have a deep need to express gratitude. To say thank you to God is part of the image of God in us. We are hard-wired as image bearers to give thanks to God. Down deep we know that God has been good to us, and we ought to give thanks.

  It has been pointed out that the problem with atheism is that the atheist has no one to thank when he feels grateful for life's good things. Imagine an atheist who has a twenty-five-year-old son who escaped the World Trade Center on September 11, 2001. Everything in him wants to thank God, but he has denied to himself that God even exists.

- Gratitude is important because it shows faith in God. Every time we say thank you to God, we express our faith. Every prayer of thanksgiving expresses our faith that God exists and that he is good and that he has been good to us. This is why Jesus says to the healed leper, who returns to say thank you, *"Your faith has made you well"* (Luke 18:42). Every prayer of gratitude shows faith.

  In *True Spirituality*, Francis Schaeffer wrote, "A quiet disposition and heart giving thanks at any given moment is the real test of the extent to which we love God at that moment."[76]

  Find yourself, every day, thanking God for his blessings. Thank him for his outrageous love for you. Thank him that he has forgiven all your sins. Thank him that you are safe in him forever. Thank him that he will never leave you or forsake you.

Thank him for a Savior. Thank him for the incarnation. Thank him for the perfect life and matchless teachings of Jesus. Thank him for a bloody cross. Thank him for the resurrection.

Thank him for the Spirit inside you and for all the ministries of the Spirit. Thank him for his power. Thank him for answered prayer. Thank him for unanswered prayer. Thank him for the Bible in your own language.

Thank him for food each day and a warm place to stay. Thank him for blue sky and brilliant moon. Thank him for people who care about you.

Thank him for the struggles of life and how he redeems those struggles. Thank him for the glory to come—glory that is far beyond your sufferings.

O give thanks to the Lord! For he is good!

- Gratitude builds faith. Giving thanks to God not only *expresses* faith but it also *builds* faith. Every day when we thank God for his marvelous blessings and gifts to us, we are reminded of God's goodness, God's love of us, God's fatherly care for us, God's grace to us, and God's provision for us. We are reminded of God's faithfulness in the past, and we are more likely to trust him for our future.

    Prayers of thanksgiving build faith.

- Gratitude is vital because grateful people are happy people. When we give thanks to God, our spirits are brightened. Our gaze is lifted from what we lack to what we have. We are more content and grateful and trusting. Clouds in our soul begin to break up and sunshine begins to break through.

A thankful spirit fosters joy and peace and contentment, and it erodes jealousy, bitterness, and gloom. Lewis Smedes, at the end of his life, wrote a remarkable statement about gratitude:

> I learned long ago that if anything can be better than getting a gift, it is the gratitude we feel for getting it. There is no other pleasure to compare with it—not sex, not winning a lottery, not hearing lovely music, not seeing stunning mountain peaks, nothing. Gratitude beats them all. I have never met a grateful person who was an unhappy person. And, for that matter, I have never met a grateful person who was a bad person.[77]

The happiest people on earth are grateful people.

Referring to the passage in Luke 17 where nine of ten lepers did not go back to Jesus to thank him for healing them, Gordon MacDonald remarked:

> The thankful spirit—the intent beneath the words—is the result of continuous discipline, because gratefulness isn't a natural or instinctive thing for most of us. Perhaps the fact that nine of the ten never came back illustrates this. Thankfulness is a learned transaction, and it comes with the realization that I neither deserve nor am entitled to blessings. At best, I am a graced recipient of all I have and am.[78]

In *A Resilient Life*, MacDonald quotes Thomas Kelly as saying:

> We pray for the big things and forget to give thanks for the ordinary, small (and yet really not small) gifts. How can God entrust great things to one who will not thankfully receive from Him the little things?[79]

Ambrose, the early church father who had a significant impact on Augustine, put it bluntly: "No duty is more urgent than that of returning thanks."[80]

In light of these five reasons, it is not surprising that Hans Selye, who did the seminal research on stress, found that the single most critical emotion for mental health was gratitude.[81] It is no wonder that an all-wise Father tells us to give thanks in everything.

Gratitude matters. It matters to God. It matters to us. It matters a lot.

Chapter 32

GREAT POWER

The prayer of a righteous person has great power as it is working.
—James 5:16

James 5:16 is a succinct sentence, full of significance. The emphasis is on the power, the great power. In the original Greek language, the first two words are "great power." Word order varies in biblical Greek, and so James is giving emphasis. He is underscoring the power of prayer—the great power of prayer. Moreover, the final word in the original is the word *effect*, translated here in the ESV *"as it is working."* It is a single word, effective. So James is emphasizing the great power of prayer and asserting that prayer is effective.

A literal translation of the five Greek words in this sentence would read: "Great power prayer righteous effective." Of course, you cannot translate literally, but if we translated somewhat literally, we could say: "Great power is the prayer of the righteous.

Effective!" More pleasing is the Christian Standard Bible's translation: *"The prayer of a righteous person is very powerful in its effect."* Prayer is very powerful. In the New International Version, this same verse reads: *"The prayer of a righteous person is powerful and effective."* Powerful and effective.

This is my point: God is dramatically underscoring in this verse the great power of prayer and the effectiveness of prayer. The sovereign God who created the universe is telling you and me that there is much power in prayer. We must never underestimate the power of prayer. Or as Charles Spurgeon put it: "Prayer is the slender nerve that moves the muscle of omnipotence."[82]

Why is God so emphatic in this brief sentence on the power of prayer? Is it because we are slow to believe it? Is it because we are reluctant to believe just how powerful prayer can be? Is it because God wants us to come into his presence and pray boldly, pray expectantly, pray frequently? This is a verse to meditate on, to chew on over and over again: *"The prayer of a righteous person is very powerful in its effect"* (CSB).

But God is not yet through with us. The Spirit inspires James to give the example of Elijah. He tells us, *"Elijah was a man with a nature like ours, and he prayed fervently that it might not rain, and for three years and six months it did not rain on the earth* (James 5:17–18).

Elijah prayed that it would not rain, and it did not rain for three and a half years. Then he prayed for rain, and the heavens opened up. God is telling us to look at this example and the power of prayer. But we might hear the satanic voice in our brains saying, "But I am not Elijah. Elijah was special. Elijah was a great prophet." And to counter that voice, God reminds us that Elijah was just a man with a nature like ours. He was a regular guy just like we are. When the verse refers to the prayer of the righteous; this does not mean the prayer of the perfect. We are righteous in the blood of Jesus. If you have trusted Christ as your Savior, then you are right with God.

It is intriguing that God chose to use the prayers of Elijah, both to stop the rain and to start the rain. He is the sovereign God, and he had determined to bring drought and then to bring downpour. He did not need the prayers of Elijah or anyone. But he chose to use those prayers.

In the same way, God chooses to use your prayers. And my prayers. So much is affected in the world through the prayers of God's people. Earlier I noted Walter Wink's assertion that "History belongs to the intercessors." [83]

One of the momentous events in my lifetime was the fall of Soviet Communism in 1989, symbolized by the fall of the Berlin Wall. There were some historical reasons for the collapse of Soviet Communism, such as the financial pressure on the Soviet economy and the firm stand of the US President Ronald Reagan. However, one day in eternity, I think we will discover that the key factor was the prayers of countless believers in Russia and Eastern Europe.

This is how you and I must view prayer: Great power! Effective!

APPENDIX A: CLASSIC PRAYERS

A Prayer of St. Patrick
Fifth century, Ireland

I arise today
Through God's strength to direct me,
God's might to uphold me,
God's wisdom to guide me,
God's eye to look before,
God's ear to hear me,
God's word to speak to me,
God's hand to guard me,
God's way to lie before me,
God's shield to protect me,
God's hosts to save me from snares of devils.
    From temptation of vices,
    From everyone who shall wish me ill,
    Afar and anear,
    Alone and in a multitude.

A Second Prayer of St. Patrick: "God Be In"
Fifth century, Ireland

God be in my head,
  And in my understanding;

God be in my eyes,
  And in my looking;

God be in my mouth;
  And in my speaking;

God be in my heart,
  And in my thinking;

God be at mind end,
  And at my departing.

A Prayer of St. Benedict
480–547, Italy

O gracious and holy Father, give us wisdom to perceive thee, diligence to seek thee, patience to wait for thee, eyes to behold thee, a heart to meditate on thee, and a life to proclaim thee; through the power of the Spirit of Jesus Christ our Lord.

A Prayer of St. Francis
1181–1226, Italy

Lord, make me an instrument of your peace:
where there is hatred, let me sow love;
where there is injury, pardon;
where there is doubt, faith;
where there is despair, hope;
where there is darkness, light;
where there is sadness, joy.
O divine Master, grant that I may not so much seek to be consoled as to console,
to be understood as to understand,
to be loved as to love.
For it is in giving that we receive,
it is in pardoning that we are pardoned,
and it is in dying that we are born to eternal life. Amen.

A Prayer of Richard of Chichester
1197–1253, England

Day by day, dear God,
of you three things we pray:
to see you more clearly,
love you more dearly,
follow you more nearly,
day by day.
Amen.

A Prayer of Lancelot Andrews
1555–1626, England

Be, Lord,
within me to strengthen me,
without me to guard me,
over me to shelter me,
beneath me to establish me,
before me to guide me,
after me to forward me,
round me to secure me.

A Prayer of John Wesley
1703–1791, England

I am no longer my own, but thine.
Put me to what thou wilt, rank me with whom
    thou wilt.
Put me to doing, put me to suffering.
Let me be employed by thee or laid aside for thee,
    exalted for thee or brought low by thee.
Let me be full, let me be empty. Let me have all
    things, let me have nothing.
I freely and heartily yield all things to thy pleasure and disposal.
And now, O glorious and blessed God, Father,
Son, and Holy Spirit,
Thou art mine, and I am thine.
So be it. Amen.

A Prayer of a Civil War Soldier

I asked for strength that I might achieve;
He made me weak that I might obey.
I asked for health that I might do great things;
He gave me grace that I might do better things.
I asked for riches that I might be happy;
I was given poverty that I might be wise.
I asked for power that I might have the praise of men;
I was given weakness that I might feel a need of God.
I asked for all things that I might enjoy life;
I was given life that I might enjoy all things.

A Prayer of John Baillie
1886–1960, Scotland

Teach me, O God, so to use all the circumstances of my life today that they may bring forth in me the fruits of holiness rather than the fruits of sin:

> Let me use disappointment as material for patience.
> Let me use success as material for thankfulness.
> Let me use trouble as material for perseverance.
> Let me use danger as material for courage.
> Let me use reproach as material for long suffering.
> Let me use praise as material for humility.
> Let me use pleasure as material for temperance.
> Let me use pain as material for endurance.

A Prayer of John Stott
1921–2011, England

The day begins for Stott at 5 a.m. He swings his legs over the side of his bed and starts the day in prayer:

> Good morning, heavenly Father; good morning, Lord Jesus; good morning, Holy Spirit.
> Heavenly Father, I worship you as the Creator and Sustainer of the universe.
> Lord Jesus, I worship you, Savior and Lord of the world.
> Holy Spirit, I worship you, Sanctifier of the people of God.
> Glory to the Father, and to the Son, and to the Holy Spirit. As it was in the beginning, is now, and will be forever. Amen.
>
> Heavenly Father, I pray that I may live this day in your presence and please you more and more.
> Lord Jesus, I pray that this day I may take up my cross and follow you.
> Holy Spirit, I pray that this day you will fill me with yourself and cause your fruit to ripen in my life: love, joy, peace, patience, kindness, goodness, faithfulness, gentleness, and self-control.
> Holy, blessed, and glorious Trinity, three persons in one God, have mercy upon me. Amen.

For decades, Stott began each day with a version of this Trinitarian prayer.

A Celtic Prayer

O Comforter! Within me as I drink my tea
Jesus! Sunlight! Offering this new morning
God of all small pleasures! Present cheerily
   Three-in-One in this glad day . . .

God of new beginnings,
   I embrace today
Jesus! Healer! Friend!
   Come sit beside me
Spirit give me power to dance
   Your merry Way
O Gentle Three-in-One
   Most Mirthful!

Ho! Ho! What a morning!

APPENDIX B: PRAISE PASSAGES

This is a list of passages in the Bible that are superb for praying back to God as part of our worship:

Exodus 34:6–8
1 Chronicles 29:10–13
Psalm 18:1–3
Psalm 27:4–8
Psalm 29:1–2
Psalm 34:1–3
Psalm 36:5–10
Psalm 42:1–2
Psalm 46:1, 7, 10–11
Psalm 47
Psalm 57:7–11
Psalm 59:16–17
Psalm 63:1–8
Psalm 66:1–5
Psalm 67
Psalm 92:1–4
Psalm 95:1–7
Psalm 96
Psalm 98
Psalm 99:1–5
Psalm 100
Psalm 103
Psalm 104:1–2, 24–35
Psalm 105:1–6
Psalm 108:1–6
Psalm 113
Psalm 115:1–3
Psalm 116:1–9

Psalm 117
Psalm 118:1, 28–29
Psalm 126
Psalm 138:1–6
Psalm 145
Psalm 147:1–7
Psalm 148
Psalm 149:1–5
Psalm 150
Isaiah 6:1–4
Isaiah 12
Isaiah 64:1–4
Lamentations 3:22–26
Zephaniah 3:14–17
John 1:1–18
Ephesians 1:3–14
Colossians 1:15–23
Hebrews 1:1–4
Revelation 1:1–20
Revelation 4:8–11
Revelation 5:8–14
Revelation 15:3–4
Revelation 19:4–16

ENDNOTES

1. Luther, Martin. *Large Catechism.* Translated by Robert H. Fischer. Philadelphia: Fortress Press, 1959.
2. Dietrich Bonhoeffer, *Life Together: The Classic Exploration of Christian Community*, trans. John W. Doberstein (HarperOne, 1954).
3. Charles Spurgeon, *Twelve Sermons on Prayer* (Baker Books, 1989), 31.
4. Phyllis Thompson, *D. E. Hoste: A Prince with God* (Kingsley Press, 2017).
5. Ole Hallesby, *Prayer*, trans. Clarence J. Carlsen (Augsburg Publishing House, 1931).
6. Jackson Senyonga, quoted in Sarona Rameka, "My Faith Journey," *https://www.saronarameka.com/faith-1*, accessed August 24, 2024.
7. George Verwer, *The Revelation of Jesus Christ Bible Reading Plan, Part 1,* YouVersion, https://www.bible.com/reading-plans/19505-the-revelation-of-jesus-christ-1/day/4.
8. Peter T. Forsyth, "Evangelical Alliance General Election 2019 Briefing," The Church of England, https://emmanuelbristol.org.uk/category/ed-shaw/page/22/.
9. A. W. Tozer, *The Knowledge of the Holy: The Attributes of God* (Harper & Row, 1978).

10. Augustine, "How Moses Saw God," YouVersion Bible Reading Plan, https://www.bible.com/reading-plans/20307-how-moses-saw-god/day/4.
11. Jonathan Edwards, "Personal Narrative (Excerpt)," *The Open Anthology of Earlier American Literature*, ed. Robin DeRosa. (Public Commons Publishing, 2015), Digital File.
12. Blaise Pascal, *Pensées*, trans. A.J. Krailsheimer (London: Penguin Books, 1995).
13. David Brainerd, quoted in "From Silence to Clarity," *Contemplate*, June 30, 2024, https://medium.com/contemplate/from-silence-to-clarity-10293aba5607, accessed August 24, 2024.
14. Frederick William Faber, Growth in Holiness; or, The Progress of the Spiritual Life (London: Richardson and Son, 1855), 148.
15. C. S. Lewis, *The Chronicle of Narnia: The Lion, the Witch and the Wardrobe* (Harper Collins Publisher, 1978), 185.
16. Gordon MacDonald, "Preserving My Unedited Thoughts," *Christianity Today*, August 13, 2003, https://www.christianitytoday.com/2003/08/cln30812/.
17. Tozer, *The Knowledge of the Holy*.
18. Oswald Chambers, *Called of God: Extracts from "My Utmost For His Highest" on the Missionary Call* (Our Daily Bread Publishing, 2015), Kindle, 19.
19. Richard J. Foster, *Prayer: Finding the Heart's True Home* (HarperOne, 1992), 165.
20. Tozer, *The Pursuit of God* (Christian Publications, 1948), 15.
21. J. Edwin Orr, *Revival and Revivalism: The Making and Marring of American Evangelicalism* (Crossway, 1986).

22. Tozer, *Pursuit of God*, 103.
23. A. T. Pierson, *The Divine Enterprise: A Study of the History of Prayer in Revival* (Fleming H. Revell, 1902).
24. Charles Spurgeon, *The Power of Prayer in the Believer's Life* (Christian Focus, 2005); originally from *Spurgeon's Sermons*, Vol. 9: 485.
25. Orr, *Revival and Revivalism*, 144.
26. Tozer, *Man: The Dwelling Place of God* (Christian Publications, 1966), 62.
27. Leonard Ravenhill, *Why Revival Tarries* (Bethany House Publishers, 1990), 27.
28. Spurgeon, *The Power of Prayer in the Believer's Life;* originally from *Spurgeon's Sermons*, Vol. 7: 329.
29. Ravenhill, 85.
30. Tony Evans, *Worship: The Ultimate Priority* (Moody Publishers, 2002).
31. Augustine, *Confessions*, trans. Edward B. Pusey (Hendrickson Publishers, 2002), 202 (Book 10, Chapter 27).
32. Augustine, *Confessions*, 202.
33. Augustine, *Confessions*, 16 (Book 1, Chapter 1).
34. Mother Teresa, *Come Be My Light: The Private Writings of the Saint of Calcutta* (Doubleday, 2007), 267.
35. Jim Elliott, *Shadow of the Almighty: The Life and Testimony of Jim Elliott*, ed. Elisabeth Elliott (Zondervan, 1958), 112.
36. Hudson Taylor, *Hudson Taylor's Spiritual Secret*, ed. Dr. and Mrs. Howard Taylor (Christian Literature Crusade, 1932).
37. John Wesley, *The Letters of John Wesley*, ed. John Telford (Epworth Press, 1931), 233.
38. Wesley, *Letters*, 256.

39. Martin Luther, *Luther's Works: Volume 48: Letters I*, ed. James Atkinson (Concordia Publishing House, 1963), 261.
40. Leon Morris, *The Gospel According to John* (Eerdmans, 1995), 19.
41. Michael Green, *The Essence of the New Testament: A Survey* (Hendrickson Publishers, 1994), 132.
42. Richard J. Foster, *Prayer: Finding the Heart's True Home* (HarperSanFrancisco, 1992), 28.
43. P. T. Forsyth, *The Soul of Prayer* (Hodder & Stoughton, 1916), 72.
44. H. B. Charles Jr, *It Happens After Prayer* (Moody Publishers, 2013), 42.
45. Billy Graham, *The Secret of Happiness* (Thomas Nelson, 2002), 121.
46. Paul Miller, *A Praying Life: Connecting with God in a Distracting World* (NavPress, 2009), 56.
47. Foster, *Prayer,* 103.
48. Augustine, *Sermons on the New Testament*, trans. Sister Marie Liguori (Fathers of the Church, 1954), 38.
49. Winston Churchill, *Never Give In: The Best of Winston Churchill's Speeches*, ed. Richard Langworth (Carroll & Graf, 2003), 132.
50. Jim Cymbala, *Fresh Wind, Fresh Fire* (Grand Rapids, MI: Zondervan, 1997), 15.
51. Jim Cymbala, *Fresh Wind, Fresh Fire* (Grand Rapids, MI: Zondervan, 1997), 55.
52. Chambers, *The Complete Works of Oswald Chambers* (Discovery House, 2000), 367.
53. Ravenhill, *Why Revival Tarries*, 93.
54. Ravenhill, *Why Revival Tarries*, 112.

55. Andrew Bonar, *The Life and Diary of David Brainerd* (Banner of Truth, 1960), 253.
56. Spurgeon, *The Power of Prayer in a Believer's Life* (Passmore & Alabaster, 1877), 24.
57. Gene Weingarten, "Pearls Before Breakfast," *The Washington Post*, April 12, 2007, C01.
58. Chambers, *My Utmost for His Highest* (Discovery House, 1992), 56.
59. Eugene Peterson, *Answering God: The Psalms as Tools for Prayer* (HarperOne, 1989), 42.
60. Andrew Murray, *With Christ in the School* (Moody Publishers, 2001), 203.
61. George Müller, *The Autobiography of George Müller*, (Whitaker House, 1984), 138.
62. Tozer, *Pursuit of God*, 49.
63. Oswald Chambers, *My Utmost for His Highest* (London: Marshall, Morgan & Scott, 1935), 22.
64. John Bunyan, *The Pilgrim's Progress*, ed. C. H. Spurgeon (The Banner of Truth Trust, 1991), 67.
65. Spurgeon, *Power of Prayer in a Believer's Life*, 55.
66. Timothy Keller, *Prayer: Experiencing Awe and Intimacy with God* (Dutton, 2014), 212.
67. Keller, *Prayer*, 212.
68. Thomas Watson, *A Body of Divinity* (Banner of Truth, 1965), 215.
69. Ann Voskamp, *The Broken Way: A Daring Path into the Abundant Life* (Zondervan, 2016), 48.
70. Thomas à Kempis, *The Imitation of Christ*, trans. L. W. Christian (Thomas Nelson, 1940), 136.

71. Alfred Lord Tennyson, *The Complete Works of Alfred Lord Tennyson*, ed. Charles Tennyson (Macmillan, 1900), 400.
72. Lewis Sperry Chafer, *Systematic Theology, Volume 4: The Doctrine of Prayer* (Dallas Seminary Press, 1947), 121.
73. William Booth, *The Salvation Army: Its Origin, Mission, and Message* (The Salvation Army, 1889), 54.
74. Walter Wink, "History Belongs to the Intercessors," in *The Powers That Be: Theology for a New Millennium* (New York: Doubleday, 1999).
75. G. K. Chesterton, *All Things Considered* (Dodd, Mead and Company, 1908), 288.
76. Francis A. Schaeffer, *True Spirituality* (Downers Grove, IL: InterVarsity Press, 1971).
77. Lewis Smedes, "God and a Grateful Old Man," in *My God and I: A Spiritual Memoir* (Grand Rapids, MI: Eerdmans, 2003), 24.
78. Gordon MacDonald, *Ordering Your Private World* (Nashville, TN: Thomas Nelson, 2003), 22.
79. Thomas Kelly, *The Eternal Promise* (Harper & Row, 1955), 49, quoted in Gordon MacDonald, *A Resilient Life: You Can Achieve Anything, and Be No One* (Thomas Nelson, 2004), 144.
80. Ambrose, *Exameron*, trans. H. de Romestin (Fathers of the Church, 1947), 102.
81. Hans Selye, *The Stress of Life* (McGraw-Hill, 1956), 279.
82. Spurgeon, *Power of Prayer in a Believer's Life*, 15.
83. Walter Wink, "History Belongs to the Intercessors," in *The Powers That Be: Theology for a New Millennium* (New York: Doubleday, 1999).

www.ingramcontent.com/pod-product-compliance
Ingram Content Group UK Ltd.
Pitfield, Milton Keynes, MK11 3LW, UK
UKHW020005160325
456262UK00006B/417

9 781632 967718